Unlock Your Deliverance

KATHRYN KRICK

Tyndale House Publishers, Carol Stream, Illinois 60188. All rights reserved.

Scripture quotations marked TPT are from The Passion Translation®. Copyright © 2017, 2018 by Passion & Fire Ministries, Inc. Used by permission. All rights reserved. ThePassionTranslation.com.

For more resources like this, visit MyCharismaShop.com and the author's website at apostlekathrynkrick.com.

Cataloging-in-Publication Data is on file with the Library of Congress.
International Standard Book Number: 978-1-63641-442-3
E-book ISBN: 978-1-63641-443-0

1 2025
Printed in the United States of America

Contents

Introduction

T EN YEARS PRIOR to my writing this, never in my
wildest dreams would I have imagined I would be
writing a book to help people receive deliverance.
A decade ago, I did not even know what deliverance
was. I was a believer my whole life. My first memory
dates back to age four, when I accepted Jesus as my Lord
and Savior. In my mid-twenties my eyes were opened
to the fact that God moves in power today, just as He
did in the Gospels and the Acts church. I witnessed
healings and demons being cast out of people, and I was
baptized in the Holy Spirit.

With my eyes now open to God's great love, I experienced Him tangibly by His power and was moved to surrender my whole life to Him. That surrender prepared me
for the divine appointment in September 2016 that would
change my life forever. Upon attending a prophetic healing
conference, a prophet named Dr. GeorDavie prophesied
that I was called to be an apostle of Jesus Christ; I was
called to reach the nations and be a vessel of God's power,
walking in miracles. Hearing this prophecy, I felt inade-
quate and unqualified. I never had a desire to preach, and
public speaking was my biggest fear and weakness. I felt
like Moses did when he said to the Lord, "Please, Lord,
I have never been a skilled speaker" (Exod. 4:10, EXB).
Nevertheless, all I wanted was to be in God's will, so I
simply obeyed and put aside my aspiration at that time of
being a Christian singer/songwriter.

I started a church (now 5F Church in Los Angeles; 5F is short for Five-Fold) nine months after receiving the prophecy, and for the first four years the church was small and actually shrank in size. All the while, I kept remembering the prophecy and trusting in God to fulfill His promise. On December 30, 2020, I posted a one-minute video on TikTok that was made up of moments where God's power moved at 5F Church. At the end of the video, I also prayed for the oppressed. This video reached one million views by my thirtieth birthday on January 1. Even more shocking, thousands of people commented about miracles they received while watching it (pain, sickness, and oppression left them).

From thereon, more of my videos went viral and miracles happened on every live stream, with a rapidly growing audience. By mid-March the church grew from a couple of people to about twenty people. On March 21, 2021, a demon manifested in a woman who traveled across the United States to attend the church. By God's grace and power, as I commanded the demon to leave the woman, it left her. This was the first demon that manifested in my ministry and the first time a demon was cast out in my ministry. A video of her deliverance went viral, and from there word spread rapidly about the deliverance taking place at 5F Church. Deliverances continued to take place each week, and by May 30 the church grew to three hundred people and revival broke out beyond our dreams.

Ever since that eventful day, people have traveled from all over the United States and all ends of the world weekly just to experience revival and encounter God's power at 5F Church in Los Angeles. This revival has expanded all around the world as I have ministered in many nations and more than one million people have watched online. Over the past few years, I have seen mass deliverance and healing take place at every event, with thousands in attendance. I'm left in awe of how massive and unlimited God's power is, as the miracles taking place at church, revival events, conferences, and online are uncountable and occur on a weekly basis. I give all glory to God and am truly shocked by what He has done in my life. I am humbled daily to be a part of His work on the earth and to serve Him.

We are living in the days our ancestors prayed for! God has brought revival to the world. He has poured out His anointing (His power) and begun the process of restoring aspects of the Acts church that have been lost by and large in the body of Christ. He has released precious "new wine" revelation that was previously replaced with "old wine" religion and churches filled with lukewarm, oppressed children of God. *Unlock Your Deliverance* is a piece of His revival. God has entrusted me with secrets of the anointing and keys of the kingdom of God that unlock deliverance for the oppressed. These precious keys are released in this book so that you may be delivered too and help others be set free.

If you are not experiencing total freedom and perhaps are even oppressed with addiction, depression, anxiety, insomnia, sickness, PTSD, effects from trauma, suicidal thoughts, stagnancy, or other issues, your time for freedom is now! If you want to help others be set free but haven't known how to help them, God is about to open your spiritual eyes and equip you to help deliver the oppressed. I am so excited for what God is going to do through these pages. I believe your life is about to change forever!

Chapter 1

WHAT IS DELIVERANCE?

WHEN YOU LOOK at the ministry of Jesus, three main components stand out: He preached about His kingdom, healed the sick, and cast out demons. In the Gospels we find Jesus constantly releasing His power to destroy the works of the devil. While sometimes that included raising the dead, it regularly involved casting out demons. Mark 1:39 describes His ministry like this: "So he traveled throughout Galilee, preaching in their synagogues and driving out demons."

He was not just preaching. He was *also* casting out demons.

Sometimes a demon spoke through a person as Jesus was preaching in a synagogue. At other times, when a demon-possessed person came near Jesus, the demons would manifest and Jesus would cast them out. In another instance a father brought his troubled child to Jesus; Jesus delivered the child from a mute demonic spirit, and the child could then speak.

Deliverance was a crucial part of Jesus' ministry. And He has called His followers—us—to do the *same works* He did (John 14:12). He commissioned His original disciples to do these works, and He is commissioning us today to do the same. "He called to him his twelve disciples and gave them authority over unclean spirits, to cast them out, and to heal every disease and every affliction" (Matt. 10:1, ESV).

Jesus even promised that "these signs will accompany those who believe: in my name they will cast out demons; they will speak in new tongues; they will pick up serpents with their hands; and if they drink any deadly poison, it will not hurt them; they will lay their hands on the sick, and they will recover" (Mark 16:17–18, ESV).

In the Book of Acts we find the disciples carrying out these words of Jesus—this Great Commission. In addition to preaching the gospel, they were constantly casting out demons, healing the sick, and at times raising the dead. The casting out of demons wasn't a minor aspect; it was just as integral to their ministry as it was to Jesus'.

There is no scripture that says, "Demons need to be cast out only in the first-century church, and then there will no longer be a need." We need deliverance today just as much as people needed it two thousand years ago in the time of Jesus and the Acts church. Jesus is the same yesterday, today, and forever (Heb. 13:8), and He cares about freeing the captives just as much in our day as He did when He walked the earth.

> The Spirit of the LORD is upon Me, because He has anointed Me to preach the gospel to the poor; He has sent Me to heal the brokenhearted, to proclaim liberty to the captives and recovery of sight to the blind, to set at liberty those who are oppressed.
> —LUKE 4:18, NKJV

What Are Demons, and Who Is the Devil?

A demon is a fallen angel. Demons are also known as "unclean spirits," "demonic spirits," and "spirits," and they are responsible for what is often called "demonic oppression." The devil, also a fallen angel, used to be the leader of worship in heaven. His leadership position there resulted in a corrupted hierarchy with his demise. In other words, he carries the most demonic supernatural power; his demons serve him and carry lesser supernatural evil powers. Still, their demonic powers can be strong on those who are not equipped and empowered to combat the devil's schemes. The power of Jesus is far higher than any power the devil or his demons have. But if believers do not access the power of Jesus, demonic power can succeed in bringing oppression in their lives. Deliverance is the casting out of a demon or demons from a person who is undergoing such satanic oppression.

The devil twists the principles of God, using them for evil. He knows that God's principles work. They are spiritual laws. For example, the principle of "Whatever one sows, that will he also reap" (Gal. 6:7, ESV) can be used for good or bad. The devil wants people to sow into evil, and in turn they will be his agents to do evil in this world. If individuals fill themselves with darkness, they will release darkness to others. This could come in many forms, such as cursing and speaking death over people or doing evil actions toward them like stealing or abusing. If one hangs around people who do evil things, that evil and demonic way of life will enter the person and they will then do evil to others.

The devil has a kingdom, just as God has a kingdom. God's kingdom brings life, but the devil's kingdom brings death. God uses angels and human vessels to carry out His works. The devil uses demons and human vessels to carry out his works. God entrusts His anointing (His power) to vessels who are surrendered to Him and have committed to serving Him. Then His vessels do as He commands, releasing the anointing to others to cast out demons, heal the sick, and preach the gospel.

The devil also uses people who are willing to serve him—usually for what they can get out of it: power, fame, money. The devil can give these things to a person for he does indeed have supernatural power. However, these "gifts" from the devil always come with sorrow, whereas gifts from God always come without sorrow.

> The blessing of the LORD makes one rich, and He adds no sorrow with it.
> —PROVERBS 10:22, NKJV

The devil's "gifts" don't come with protection; they can be taken at any moment. And they can come with demons—making the recipient unable to enjoy these "gifts" because of the torment. The devil may also demand an evil sacrifice from a person who receives his "gifts."

When the devil uses people as vessels or agents, they become witches and warlocks. The terms *witch* and *warlock* describe those who use demonic powers to accomplish the devil's agenda. Witches and warlocks indeed exist today; they're not just make-believe characters we see in movies and books. They are undercover for the most part because the truth of what they do would not be enticing to society at large.

The devil wins only through lies and deception. Witches and warlocks deceive others, making it seem as though what they're doing is good when really they are releasing demons. For example, a psychic is actually a witch using demonic supernatural powers to access secrets about a person's life. A demon can follow a person around and learn their habits and details about their life. Then that demon will report to the psychic as the person is sitting there getting their "reading." When anyone goes to a psychic, they are technically giving demonic powers access to speak into their life. In the spiritual realm that action opens the door and gives the enemy authority to bring demonic oppression. So, some demons come to people through psychics. A psychic never helps a person but actually releases a demon to them.

The devil's kingdom is made up of demons and agents of demons (witches and warlocks) who carry out his works. His agenda is the opposite of God's. The devil's kingdom brings death and seeks to steal, kill, and destroy (John 10:10).

The biggest work of the devil—where he's the most successful—is when demons enter people. For instance, when a demon of addiction enters a person, that person has now become oppressed, and it's as if a demonic chain is wrapped around them. If they have just one demon of addiction, they will find that in that area (drugs, drinking, masturbation, sex, food, watching porn, and so forth) they absolutely cannot control themselves. Most people who have demonic spirits of addiction want to stop doing the addictive behaviors, but no matter how hard they try, they cannot quit. The same goes for other areas of demonic oppression. For example, when a demon of depression enters a person, the demon has control of the person's thoughts, sometimes leading to lack of energy, various forms of self-harm, thoughts of suicide, a desire to "check out" of life, and so forth.

The lives of many successful people have taken a turn for the worse because addiction overtook them. Most of these people truly loved their careers and blessings and didn't want to ruin them with drugs, alcohol, and so on. Others gave into suicidal thoughts or were constantly depressed, no matter how many good things happened to them. Most of them would have preferred to stop the suicidal thoughts rather than end their lives. But they had absolutely no control. These are all results of demonic oppression. This is why the devil works day and night to oppress anyone he can. This is where he has power over people.

Isaiah 10:27 says, "The yoke shall be destroyed because of the anointing" (KJV). And Jesus came to destroy the works of the devil (1 John 3:8). On the cross Jesus destroyed the curse that gave the devil power over humanity. Now whoever believes that Jesus is Lord receives eternal life and an abundant life here and now (John 10:10). This includes an inheritance from God.

> If [we are His] children, [then we are His] heirs also: heirs of God and fellow heirs with Christ [sharing His spiritual blessing and inheritance], if indeed we share in His suffering so that we may also share in His glory.
>
> —ROMANS 8:17, AMP

Jesus has healing. Jesus has freedom. Jesus has abundant life. Jesus has supernatural resources from heaven. We therefore receive the same as coheirs with Christ. God made this even clearer in another scripture:

> He was wounded for our transgressions, He was bruised for our iniquities; the chastisement for our peace *was* upon Him, and by His stripes we are healed.
>
> —ISAIAH 53:5, NKJV

Before Jesus went to the cross, He began to shed blood for our healing through the scourging He endured. Scourging involved being whipped with a brutal instrument made of leather straps with sharp objects on the ends that pulled the flesh out. Though this is graphic to read, it's necessary for you to understand the price Jesus paid so you could be healed today. We should take seriously what Jesus has done for us and never take our inheritance from God lightly but rather treat it with reverence and honor. Today as Christians we believe that healing—which includes freedom—is our right as children of God. It's as if this "inheritance clause" is in a contract that God has signed. This inheritance belongs to us!

When a person becomes a believer in Jesus, in the spiritual realm they receive this inheritance. Now they can receive healing and freedom. The demons have to leave them. However, demons don't generally leave the moment a person is saved, although that can happen. Usually demons leave as the person accesses their inheritance from God according to His principles. Delivering His people from demons is one of God's principles, and He uses His anointed vessels to accomplish this. These men and women of God walk in the authority He has given them and command the demons to leave individuals.

We see this principle first in Jesus' ministry. As we noted earlier, Scripture says He would preach *and* cast out demons. Jesus didn't just preach and do an altar call, and then the people repented and demons automatically left. In addition to preaching repentance, Jesus also executed His authority over the demons, and they would flee.

We also see this principle in the Acts church. Jesus told the disciples/apostles to preach that the kingdom of heaven was at hand *and* to cast out demons (Matt. 10:7–8).

He never told people to cast demons out of themselves; He told them to cast demons out of others. This shows us that God's principle is for people to seek deliverance by positioning themselves where the anointing is flowing so that the yoke in their lives may be destroyed. When they do as God commanded and meet together as believers (Heb. 10:25), whether physically, online, or in revival meetings and services, they will encounter the anointing that flows through vessels and destroys yokes. And they will be set free! So, today Jesus is still destroying the works of the devil as He moves through anointed vessels, setting the captives free.

In the next chapter we will discuss why deliverance is so needed today.

Chapter 2

WHY DELIVERANCE IS NEEDED TODAY

S O MANY ISSUES that people face today are demonic, and many do not realize it. The devil has worked hard to push a false narrative that deliverance is not necessary and that it is "weird," "scary," and only for rare circumstances such as the extremely possessed people portrayed in horror movies that show exorcism. When demons aren't exposed, they can stay and keep oppressing people. It is only when a believer embraces the anointing and walks boldly in their authority in Christ that demons are exposed and have to leave.

During Jesus' earthly ministry, when He was present, demons would expose themselves, speaking out or physically manifesting in people. Demons also manifested in the presence of the apostles and other fivefold ministers in the Acts church. Jesus and the ministers in the Acts church all carried true anointing and walked in authority, boldly and unashamedly confronting demons. When ministers do not embrace the anointing and the ministry of deliverance, the anointing will not come. God does not force Himself. When ministers reject the anointing, demons will hide in people. People in the church may lift their hands in worship, say "Hallelujah," and never miss a Sunday while demons sit comfortably inside them. It is the *anointing* that destroys the yoke, not attending any church, listening to a message, or singing worship songs.

CAN CHRISTIANS HAVE DEMONS?

Yes, Christians can have demons. When you give your life to Jesus, your spirit comes alive and is inhabited by the Holy Spirit. You are "born again" because your spirit is co-resurrected with Christ. You are literally a new creation, but you don't automatically become a completely new person. You don't get a new body and a new soul.

You are made up of three parts: spirit, soul, and body. Your soul comprises your mind, will, and emotions. Your memories, ways of thinking, desires, and natural feelings don't get wiped away when you give your life to Jesus. Your soul doesn't become new upon salvation. Your soul has to be transformed, and that transformation takes place as you continually surrender to God and obey Him, which includes following the principles in His Word. Here is an example of how your mind will transform as you follow His principles.

> Do not conform to the pattern of this world, but be transformed by the renewing of your mind. Then you will be able to test and approve what God's will is—his good, pleasing and perfect will.
> —ROMANS 12:2

When your mind is thinking carnally (how it always has in the past), be intentional about renewing your mind by reading the Word and meditating on it. As you make meditating on the Word of God a regular part of your life, your mind will be transformed. You will start automatically thinking like Christ and seeing circumstances through His perspective. But this doesn't happen on day one of becoming a believer.

When you first become a believer, your soul needs a deep cleaning. You may have wrong, carnal ways of thinking. Bad emotions may be flowing regularly from your soul: anger, hatred, bitterness, unforgiveness, jealousy, lust. And there may also be demons that need to be evicted.

Please understand: Demons cannot live in your spirit, where the Holy Spirit dwells. However, demons can live in your soul. It's like the Holy Spirit lives with your spirit in the bedroom of the house. The bedroom is immaculate, perfectly clean. Yet the kitchen and bathroom are dirty. You may need to clean the other "rooms" in your soul regarding your thoughts and behavior. You may need to stop swearing. You may need to stop meditating on things of darkness—such as lusting after people, thinking hateful thoughts toward another, and always focusing on the negative. You may need to stop doing drugs, sleeping around, or gambling. And an even deeper cleaning may need to take place: evicting demons. It may not only be "trash and dust bunnies" you need to get rid of. There may also be "cockroaches" that need exterminating.

Once you accept Jesus as Lord, the Holy Spirit is your helper, and as you allow Him, He will help you in every area. So, a demon cannot control you as a person— meaning a demon cannot totally possess you as if you're a robot. However, if you are oppressed by a demon in an area of addiction, the demon controls that area until you receive deliverance.

A man who came to my church testified that he had a porn addiction as a believer for decades. He read his Bible often, prayed, fasted, had accountability partners, and did just about everything possible to get rid of this addiction.

But the addiction remained. Many people made him feel as if he were the issue—his heart wasn't good enough, or he wasn't doing enough. One day he watched a video from my church, 5F Church (Five-Fold Church), and the power of God came through the screen and delivered him. The addiction was totally gone. Years have passed since then, and he hasn't struggled with pornography at all. Prior to the deliverance, he was a true believer and was filled with the Holy Spirit, yet this one area of his life was controlled by the demonic spirit. But as he sought the Holy Spirit for help, the Holy Spirit led him to where the anointing—the power of God—was being released, and the man was set free!

Rather than get hung up on the arguments of "Can a believer have demons?" or "Is it *oppressed* or *possessed*?" why don't we focus on the depraved state of the people who need freedom? While theological debates rage about this topic, the devil is laughing at the religious debaters, who are allowing the oppressed to stay in bondage by not embracing the anointing and the ministry of deliverance. The current state of the body of Christ is very simple and urgent: God's people must be free!

HOW TO KNOW IF I HAVE A DEMON

When it seems as if a force is controlling you in a certain area, that is an indication of demonic oppression. Most addicted people don't want to continue in their addictions, but there is a force that controls them. Have you ever known a Christian who had an addiction and genuinely did everything in their power to stop it, seeking God earnestly, but could not? That Christian most likely had a spirit of addiction. Yes, addiction is a demon.

Depression is a demonic spirit also. Have you ever known a Christian who couldn't shake depression no matter how many times they did all that God said to do, renewing their mind with the Word and declaring "Jesus has given me perfect peace"? That Christian probably had a spirit of depression.

Have you ever known a Christian who was overtaken by anxiety attacks, even though they were truly surrendered to God and meditated on His Word, quoting "God did not give me a spirit of fear" over and over? That Christian most likely had a spirit of anxiety.

There's a difference between needing to be delivered and needing to crucify your flesh. Feeling anxious at times is not a demon. However, *anxiety* is a demonic spirit. Feeling sad and down sometimes is not a demon. However, *depression* is a demonic spirit. Having cravings that you could control if you wanted to is not a demon. However, *addiction* is a demonic spirit. Allowing your flesh to dominate is not the same as having a yoke that can be destroyed only by the anointing. Still, demons have hidden in people for so long because the devil has tricked us into thinking that *nothing* is a demon and that instead we "just need to stop sinning."

There are yokes on God's people that need to be destroyed, and this can be done only by the anointing. Yes, crucifying your flesh is vital. It's by renewing your mind with God's Word and choosing God's will over the devil's that you keep doors shut to the devil and stay free. But when a demon is already there, deliverance is needed.

The doctrine that says Christians cannot have demons is wrong. The true doctrine is this: Christians cannot have demons *when* they have followed God's principles to clean their souls (which, for many, includes receiving deliverance) and live lives surrendered to Jesus, closing all doors to the devil. When you do this, a demon cannot enter you. You are completely protected! Yet prior to encountering the anointing and receiving proper spiritual equipping through the fivefold ministry, believers may be oppressed by demons—as many are today due to a lack of these essentials in the body of Christ.

INSTANCES WHERE CHRISTIANS MAY HAVE DEMONS

Demons enter a person when the person gives them authority. The devil did not have power until Adam and Eve handed over their God-given authority by obeying him rather than God. As soon as they handed their authority to the devil, he gained access and power over their lives.

God gives us free will. We can do the same thing Adam and Eve did if we choose. Jesus has given us authority over the enemy, but we can choose to hand it over to the enemy if we want. Going against God's commands is the action of following the enemy's voice instead of God's; it is the action of giving authority to the devil rather than to God. When you do what God says, it's as if you're saying, "I give You authority over my life. Your will be done. You are my master and leader." When you do what the enemy says, it's like saying, "I'm choosing to do what you want; therefore, I'm giving you authority to be my leader."

So, in the spiritual realm, simply by disobeying God, a person opens a door to the devil, giving him access and permission to do what he wants. And what he wants is to fill the person with demons, as that is how he then imprisons and controls them.

Before salvation, people may have opened the "doors" of their souls to spirits of addiction by indulging in drugs, pornography, gambling, and so on. They might have allowed spirits of rage to enter because they followed their emotions and lashed out at anyone they felt anger toward. Sometimes a person may experience deliverance immediately upon being saved. Jesus can deliver a person however He wants, and we should never put Him in a box by saying, "He can deliver someone only this way." However, most testimonies I've heard sound like this: "Upon salvation my life changed as I fell in love with Jesus and His Spirit entered my life. Loneliness went away as I found a friend in Jesus, and I experienced peace, joy, hope, and contentment for the first time in my life. But the addiction (or anxiety, rage, nightmares, insomnia, etc.) remained." Can you relate?

Many of these struggles persist after a person's salvation because deliverance is still needed. Salvation and deliverance are two separate things. Jesus is our Savior, Healer, Deliverer, and giver of abundant life. You receive the gift of Jesus and what He provides by faith in Him. The problem is that many people have faith in Jesus the Savior but not in Jesus the Deliverer. A big reason for this is that, by and large, the news hasn't gotten out that Jesus can deliver—that Jesus can and wants to deliver you from every kind of oppression.

> So then faith comes by hearing, and hearing by the word of God.
>
> —ROMANS 10:17, NKJV

People need to hear from Christian leaders and all believers that Jesus is their Savior *and* Deliverer and Healer so they can then have faith to receive the deliverance and healing. Some of God's people are being destroyed by demons oppressing them because they lack the knowledge about Jesus the Deliverer.

> My people are destroyed for lack of knowledge.
> —HOSEA 4:6, NKJV

Christians can have demons as the result of two things: (1) they had demons prior to salvation, and since being saved, they have yet to experience deliverance, many times because they have not encountered the anointing that destroys the yoke; and (2) after salvation they opened doors to demons.

As I said previously, all of us are given free will. When you follow God's commands in His Word (with the proper revelation from the Holy Spirit) and truly live surrendered to God, you will not open doors to demons, and therefore demons *cannot* enter you. No Christian should be afraid that a demon will enter them, but instead they should have the *fear of God*, remembering that the rewards of freedom and protection from demons come from living surrendered to Him. In short, if you surrender to God and obey Him, demons cannot enter you! But if you choose, out of your own free will, to open a door through disobedience, a demon could enter you, even if you call yourself a Christian and the Holy Spirit lives in you.

Most people who think that Christians can't have demons probably don't understand what demons truly are and how common they are. Addiction is a demonic stronghold; it is not a person's lack of self-control. All drugs can have an addictive nature, which is actually mobilized by a demonic influence. Many a person whose drug addiction is destroying their life strongly desires to stop doing drugs. Yet how many examples have you seen or heard where no matter how hard a person tried to quit, they couldn't? When this is the case, it is absolutely a spirit of addiction.

If a person—whether nonbeliever or believer—takes drugs every day, they will get addicted. Being addicted means having a spirit of addiction. A Christian isn't immune from getting a demon of addiction just because they're a Christian. It's up to them to obey God or not. That is one of the simplest explanations of how a believer can have a demon—and of why it is so common today for Christians to be oppressed by demons.

Many believers open doors to demons by disobeying God in certain areas. Some choose to be lukewarm. For others, the reason is the lack of anointing in the church today that is necessary to release God's kingdom on believers. Paul said, "My message and my preaching were not with wise and persuasive words, but with a demonstration of the Spirit's power, so that your faith might not rest on human wisdom, but on God's power" (1 Cor. 2:4–5). Some people are living lukewarm lives, disobeying God and opening doors to the devil, not because they have a bad heart but because they have yet to encounter God's power, which opens spiritual eyes and builds a true faith in Him.

A faith that rests on God's power rather than on man's words is a strong, true faith that leads to real repentance and surrender. The power of God is needed for spiritual eyes to open to the magnitude of God's love. With the revelation of God's love and worthiness, one will then be compelled and strongly desire to live a life pleasing to Him every day.

Christians can have demons simply because doors were

opened at some point in their lives. Somewhere along the way authority was given to the enemy. These doors could have been opened before salvation, after salvation, or in prior generations. I'll go more in-depth on this topic of doors that demons enter through in chapter 3.

Deliverance isn't just some side ministry for people who have dabbled in witchcraft, have bloodshot eyes, and are foaming at the mouth like "possession" movies depict. Deliverance isn't just for charismatic Christians who are "into that stuff" and feel called to that kind of ministry. Deliverance is desperately needed in *every* church.

Jesus the Savior is the answer to everyone's problems and the only way to find true and eternal life. And deliverance—or, more specifically, Jesus the Deliverer—is the answer to most people's problems. Again, Jesus came to save us *and* deliver us. We as the body of Christ cannot choose which parts of Jesus we like and disregard the rest. There shouldn't be "the church that does deliverance ministry," "the church that does healing ministry," and "the church that does teaching ministry." Jesus has commanded that we do it all. The blueprint of what church should look like is found in the Book of Acts, and that church did all of these. That's because all three of these ministries are vital to showing the love of Jesus to people. We can't show just one-third of Jesus to the world. We need to reveal all of Him.

God's people need to be free! So many children of God are missing out on this precious, costliest gift that Jesus paid the price for: healing, freedom, and abundant life. This grieves God deeply. He loves His children so much that He sacrificed His life and went through the worst punishment so they could be free from the devil's grip, yet so many aren't receiving this gift!

We need to do better as the body of Christ. We need to have more of the fear of God and humility to hear what He is speaking right now. The Lord wants His people set free! He wants us to accept His anointing and the ministry of deliverance, even if it's out of our comfort zone. Even if it means the Pharisees of today hurl insults at you, falsely accuse you, and leave your church or your life. Even if it gets messy with demons manifesting through coughs, screams, glares, and resistance. Even if it means you'll be misunderstood and lose friends. We need to embrace deliverance in the body of Christ so that God's people can receive their full inheritance and be free from the chains of the devil.

We also need deliverance to be accepted and embraced by the body of Christ because true salvation of people depends on it. True salvation doesn't come from entertainment and a persuasive message at church. It comes by encountering God in power and truly meeting Jesus. The more that ministry looks the way Paul demonstrated it—releasing the anointing to people rather than speaking in fancy words— the more souls will be saved. As we shine brightly for Jesus, we attract the lost to Him (Matt. 5:14–16). The way to truly be a bright light for Jesus is to walk in the abundant life He provided and thereby reflect His glory and the supernatural life (heaven on earth) that comes on a believer.

But for all this to happen, one must first be set free from demons. A person under demonic oppression is in "the negatives," so to speak. Once the person is delivered, they reset to zero, and from there they go "from glory to glory" into "the positives" as God's abundant life in them increases. For example, a person may move from having a spirit of depression and being tired most of the time (in the negatives) to being set free—no longer depressed and no longer tired (at zero)—to then having supernatural, abundant joy and energy (in the positives).

When oppressed and lost people see your supernatural life shining so bright, they are attracted! They are attracted to the Jesus in you. They will be moved to ask you why your life is so supernatural and abundant. They will be hungry to discover where you've found this life and to desire it for themselves. Being delivered and walking in our full inheritance of abundant life in Christ is how we will be most effective in the kingdom of God—seeing souls saved, delivered, and transformed!

Chapter 3

HOW DEMONIC
OPPRESSION HAPPENS

MANY BELIEVERS MISTAKENLY believe that since God is so loving, a person can just live however they want "as long as they mean well," and they will be completely protected. Some believers think that just because they confess Jesus as their Lord, go to church, and occasionally read the Bible, no demon can touch them. But the reality is that you can't separate God from His Word. He is the Word. And you can't separate the Word from the "new wine" revelation that comes when one seeks the Holy Spirit to bring understanding.

One day the disciples of John the Baptist came to Jesus and asked him, "Why don't your disciples fast like we do and the Pharisees do?" Jesus replied, "Do wedding guests mourn while celebrating with the groom? Of course not. But someday the groom will be taken away from them, and then they will fast. Besides, who would patch old clothing with new cloth? For the new patch would shrink and rip away from the old cloth, leaving an even bigger tear than before. And no one puts new wine into old wineskins. For the old skins would burst from the pressure, spilling the wine and ruining the skins. New

wine is stored in new wineskins so that both are
preserved."

—MATTHEW 9:14–17, NLT

In this scripture Jesus compares the Pharisees and John
the Baptist's revelation of fasting to "old wine." And He
compares His revelation of how to fast to "new wine."
Jesus came with a new way. The Pharisees did not have
the true revelation of God's Word when it came to fasting
as well as many other spiritual principles and instructions
from God in His Word.

The new wine (proper revelation from God) was
needed to bring salvation and the kingdom of heaven to
earth. The Pharisees interpreted the Word of God one
way, and Jesus interpreted it another. The "religious revelation" of the Word of God is what accused and crucified
Jesus. The revelation from the Holy Spirit (new wine) that
Jesus revealed set people free and saved them.

When a church is missing certain aspects of the Acts
church such as the power of God, the casting out of
demons, and the healing of the sick, it also means that
new wine revelation is missing as well. We must have
understanding from God on how to access His kingdom
and how to adequately operate in His anointing to do His
works.

Throughout this book I mention new wine often.
Whenever you see the term *new wine*, know that it means
the revelation Jesus brought that by and large has been
lost. This revelation includes the realities of the spiritual
realm—the deeper things, or "mysteries," of the kingdom
of God that are needed to execute authority over demonic
powers and release God's kingdom to the earth.

I will walk in freedom, for I have devoted myself to
your commandments.
—PSALM 119:45, NLT

Therefore, get rid of all moral filth and the evil that
is so prevalent and humbly accept the word planted
in you, which can save you.

Do not merely listen to the word, and so deceive
yourselves. Do what it says. Anyone who listens
to the word but does not do what it says is like
someone who looks at his face in a mirror and, after
looking at himself, goes away and immediately for-
gets what he looks like. But whoever looks intently
into the perfect law that gives freedom, and continues in it—not forgetting what they have heard,
but doing it—they will be blessed in what they do.
—JAMES 1:21–25

These scriptures tell us that freedom comes when you
devote yourself to the commandments in the Word and
that "the perfect law...gives freedom." Salvation comes
when "you declare with your mouth, 'Jesus is Lord,' and
believe in your heart that God raised him from the dead"
(Rom. 10:9). And the true salvation that you can be confident in requires *true surrender*. It's not up to any of us on
earth to speculate who will or won't go to heaven based on
whether we think they're lukewarm or surrendered. Only
God knows. However, we do know that we can be confident in our salvation and pleasing to God only if we surrender our whole lives.

> For wide is the gate and broad is the road that leads
> to destruction, and many enter through it. But
> small is the gate and narrow the road that leads to
> life, and only a few find it.
> —MATTHEW 7:13–14

The narrow gate of surrender is not only where true salvation is found; it is also the only place where abundant life is found. John 10:10 says, "The thief comes only in order to steal and kill and destroy. I came that they may have and enjoy life, and have it in abundance [to the full, till it overflows]" (John 10:10, AMP).

The Bible says we have an inheritance as children of God:

> For his Spirit joins with our spirit to affirm that we
> are God's children. And since we are his children,
> we are his heirs. In fact, together with Christ we
> are heirs of God's glory. But if we are to share his
> glory, we must also share his suffering.
> —ROMANS 8:16–17, NLT

The inheritance you have received is a life of abundance, including healing and deliverance (Isa. 53:5), a sound mind (2 Tim. 1:7, NKJV), peace (Isa. 26:3), provision (Phil. 4:19), and protection (John 10:27–29). Many Christians don't realize they actually have an inheritance, so because of a lack of knowledge, they are not receiving what is already theirs (Hos. 4:6, NKJV).

The road map to deliverance, healing, and abundant life is all in the Word of God, but with true revelation coming from the Holy Spirit. One way to discover the Holy Spirit's voice in the Word is to position yourself to receive vital equipping from the fivefold ministry—apostles, prophets, evangelists, pastors, and teachers (Eph. 4:11–16). God has gifted apostles with a special grace to understand the Word of God and teach it. This is what I am doing in this book. When you seek the Lord with all your heart, you will find Him (Jer. 29:13). By reading this book, you are seeking the Lord, and you will find Him! You will find more revelation of His Word, which will lead to accessing more of God and His blessings in your life.

PRINCIPLES IN THE SPIRITUAL REALM

God is a God of principles. The spiritual realm and the kingdom of God operate by various laws: when you do _____, you will get _____. For instance, what you sow, you will reap. If you are generous, supernatural provision will come to you (Gal. 6:7–9; Mal. 3:10). Another principle is that if you speak words of life aligned with God's will, you will receive abundant life, but if you speak words of death, you block the blessings from God and can even be responsible for bringing problems in your life (Prov. 18:21). These are just a couple of examples of the many principles found in the Word of God.

One of the main principles you must know to receive deliverance and healing is this: When you follow God's Word, you will receive salvation and access your inheritance from God (healing, deliverance, peace, sound mind, protection, and provision).

God does not go against His Word. You can't receive deliverance and healing any way you want. They come when you follow God's principles as revealed in His Word. For the most part, the main reason people are oppressed, while praying to be free and trying what they think are spiritual things, is simply that they are not following God's principles.

> Now I say to you that you are Peter (which means "rock"), and upon this rock I will build my church, and all the powers of hell will not conquer it. And I will give you the keys of the Kingdom of Heaven. Whatever you forbid on earth will be forbidden in heaven, and whatever you permit on earth will be permitted in heaven.
>
> —Matthew 16:18–19, nlt

The authority of the *keys* here is ultimately in the revelation of God's principles from the Scriptures. Revelation of God's Word, when applied, unlocks deliverance! God is presently using apostles and all fivefold ministry offices. The keys of the kingdom have been released today. And the keys that unlock deliverance are found in this book!

Principle of Free Will

> The Lord God commanded the man, "You are free to eat from any tree in the garden; but you must not eat from the tree of the knowledge of good and evil, for when you eat from it you will certainly die."
>
> —Genesis 2:16–17

> This day I call the heavens and the earth as witnesses against you that I have set before you life and death, blessings and curses. Now *choose life*, so that you and your children may live.
>
> —Deuteronomy 30:19, emphasis added

God says you can choose life or death, blessings or curses. He advises you to choose life, but the choice is yours. God told Adam, "You are free to eat from any tree of the garden." In the same way, there is absolute free will for us today. We can choose (1) life and blessings or (2) death and curses. We receive life by being surrendered to God and following His Word (according to new-wine revelation). Death comes by doing the opposite: being disobedient and disregarding the Word of God.

> You He made alive, who were dead in trespasses and sins, in which you once walked according to the course of this world, according to the prince of the power of the air, the spirit who now works in the sons of disobedience, among whom also we all once conducted ourselves in the lusts of our flesh, fulfilling the desires of the flesh and of the mind, and were by nature children of wrath, just as the others.
> —Ephesians 2:1–3, nkjv

Because the devil is still in the world as the "ruler" (John 16:11, nkjv) and prince of the power of the air, if a person of their own free will decides to live in disobedience, the devil will be at work in them. This is a spiritual law: if a person, whether a believer or not, decides to be disobedient and disregard God's Word, the devil is allowed to bring oppression—to send a demonic spirit to them.

> Do not give the devil a foothold.
> —Ephesians 4:27

Open Door of Sin

When a door in the spiritual realm is opened to him, the devil has legal access to go through that door, and demons have the legal right to enter the person. Demonic oppression always occurs because a door has been opened. One main way that doors open to evil in the spiritual realm is through a person's sin. This is what it means to "give the devil a foothold." Instead of locking the door, the person opens the door by sinning; then the devil can put his foot between the doorframe and the door and come in.

To keep these doors shut, you must be conscientious and take your spiritual health seriously. You have to desire to please God more than anything else. Just as you diligently lock the door of your house because you value your physical safety and possessions, you also must value your spiritual health, blessings, and relationship with God and always keep the spiritual doors shut to the devil, never allowing him access.

Leaving your house door unlocked and cracked open doesn't necessarily mean a robber will come inside, but it is now possible. The same is true in the spiritual realm. Opening a door through sin doesn't guarantee that the person will immediately get a demon, but that is now a possibility. The longer the door stays open and the more often additional doors are opened through sinning in other areas, the greater the chances that demonic spirits will enter.

The likelihood of a demonic spirit entering through the open door also has to do with a person's own or generational past. If you've caught the devil's attention as an easy target because of doors you've opened in the past and/or doors your parents have opened, the chances of a demonic spirit entering increase.

Spirits of addiction

When a person disobeys God by getting drunk, they may not receive a spirit of addiction right away. But in many cases as the door remains open through habitual drunkenness, a spirit of addiction will enter. A spirit of addiction may oppress a person by way of many different things: alcohol, drugs, sex, porn, masturbation, social media, TV, sugar, food, caffeine, and more. If you're depending on something more than God for pleasure, energy, or fulfillment, you are opening a door for the spirit of addiction.

Spirits of rage

Giving in to the temptation of acting out in anger opens the door to a spirit of rage. Many people who continually inflict verbal and/or physical abusive on their loved ones have spirits of rage. The first time they see that they've caused harm by acting out their anger and being abusive, many individuals never want to act that way again or cause their loved ones more pain. But when a person has a demonic spirit of rage, once the feeling of anger comes, that spirit controls them. It doesn't make logical sense why a person would repeatedly abuse a loved one. The truth is that it's spiritual.

Spiritual spouses and sexual spirits

Impure sexual spirits and spiritual spouses come when people open doors through sexual acts outside marriage and impure sexual behavior such as masturbating and watching porn. These impure sexual spirits give a person strong sexual impulses and thoughts. A spiritual spouse is a demonic spirit that typically comes in the night and touches a person sexually and/or gives them impure sexual dreams. A spiritual spouse gets jealous and does not want the person it is oppressing to have another partner, so it will usually work to bring division in a marriage or romantic relationship. Many times married couples struggle with physical and emotional intimacy because of a spiritual spouse that one or both of them have.

Demonic soul ties

Some demonic oppression comes from having demonic soul ties. A demonic soul tie occurs when there is a close, ungodly connection between two people. The main example of an ungodly soul tie is when one person is manipulating another. Sometimes a person who is disobedient to God uses manipulation tactics to try to make sure a romantic partner or friend never leaves them, is afraid to displease them, and will do anything for this person.

Signs that you have a demonic soul tie with someone include feeling controlled by them (and only by them). Maybe you don't usually care what people think about you, but when it comes to this person, you feel as though you have no choice but to do what they say and you care a great deal about what they think of you. Another example is when you know you shouldn't be with a person romantically, but you feel you can't leave them—or if you break up, you keep getting back together. Doors for demonic soul ties open when you give in to manipulation repeatedly and/or when you date or maintain a close friendship with a person even though you know God doesn't want you to.

OPEN DOOR OF SPEAKING DEATH

Another open door to demons is speaking words of death.

Death and life are in the power of the tongue, and
those who love it and indulge it will eat its fruit and
bear the consequences of their words.

—PROVERBS 18:21, AMP

One of the biggest schemes of the enemy is to bring lies
to your mind—lies about your identity, the character of
God, your inheritance as a child of God, and your future.
The devil's aim is to get you to believe those lies so you
will then speak them. Once you speak the lies, in the spiritual realm it's the action of agreement. If you say, "I want
to die," it's counted as accepting what the devil is saying
and allowing him to have authority in this situation. The
devil then has spiritual legal authority to put his "foot" in
the foothold and send demonic spirits to bring constant
thoughts telling a person they should kill themselves.

We are called to resist the devil's lies and take every
thought captive (Jas. 4:7; 2 Cor. 10:5). We are not supposed to speak everything we feel as if it's our truth.
When you declare the devil's lies as if they are the truth
and your portion, you are giving him a foothold. For
example, when a person says, "I have bad anxiety," they
are agreeing with the devil's lie rather than rejecting the
lie and speaking the truth: "God did not give me a spirit
of fear" (see 2 Timothy 1:7, NKJV) and "I have perfect peace
because my mind is stayed on You" (see Isaiah 26:3, NKJV).

The Bible says that by His stripes we are healed (Isa.
53:5). If you receive a bad diagnosis, the spiritually right
way to speak about it is to speak aloud that you reject this
sickness or pain and declare, "I am healed by Jesus' stripes."
You can tell others, "The doctor has diagnosed me with
_____," rather than confessing over and over again, "I
have _____." This way there is no foothold for the devil.

THE MOST OVERLOOKED YET MOST COMMON DISOBEDIENCE

Choosing to disobey God and disregard His Word can take other forms than sinning by doing drugs, sleeping around, engaging in witchcraft, stealing, lying, or committing adultery. It can also look like keeping pride in your heart. Or it may involve leading a "comfortable" Christian life in a lukewarm church when God is calling you to pick up your cross of discomfort and persecution and follow Him, accepting the Holy Spirit in all the ways He works—even through unlikely vessels who move in power that makes demons leave.

Many believers are missing freedom and abundant life because they're standing *beside* God's will but not *in* God's will. They're doing all the right Christian things except embracing the current move of God—the revival of the anointing, deliverance, and new-wine revelation through His apostles and prophets. This is where the keys of the kingdom are being released.

> Believe in the LORD your God, and you shall be established; believe His prophets, and you shall prosper.
>
> —2 CHRONICLES 20:20, NKJV

To prosper, you need to accept God's way of releasing revelation of His Word, the keys of the kingdom, and the anointing that destroys the yoke through anointed leaders such as prophets and apostles.

OPEN DOOR OF ABUSE

The open doors of sin, including speaking words of death, are doors we each have control over. Many people are oppressed because they chose to give the devil a foothold and thus got themselves into these situations. However, many also *unknowingly* give the devil a foothold simply because they don't have the spiritual knowledge, understanding, and wisdom. This again proves the importance of accepting God's system of equipping believers through the fivefold ministry. Lukewarm, milky teaching keeps believers bound because of their lack of knowledge.

There are other ways doors can open to the devil that people do not open themselves. It is wrong to think that because someone is oppressed, they must have sinned. Many times, that is not the case. One clear example is the open door of abuse. For instance, when a child is abused sexually, the traumatic experience often leads to the devil planting lies about their identity and lies of shame. Many individuals have testified that they started experiencing lustful, romantic desires at a young age right after they were sexually abused.

When spiritually equipped, even at a young age, a person can discern the devil's schemes after the abuse, recognizing these impure thoughts as lies of the devil and therefore rejecting them. But when someone does not have this equipping, they will often speak aloud and act on the thoughts they are having. And the moment they do that, they've given the devil a foothold. So, some people have open doors to the enemy as a direct result of being abused.

OPEN DOOR OF GENERATIONAL CURSES

Another kind of open door that is out of a person's control is generational sins. Repetitive sins in their family lineage can lead to a person's demonic oppression. The more doors that are open and the more one delves into the kingdom of darkness, the deeper the bondage will grow.

One example of deeper bondage is a generational curse. A person may experience oppression even from a young age simply because of a generational curse passed down from their ancestors. For example, with a generational curse of rage and abuse, one might have a natural inkling to be rageful and abusive even at an early age. They have this tendency because oppression is already there, through the generational curse.

Chapter 4

WHAT MAKES DEMONS GO—
KEY 1: THE ANOINTING

T HE ANOINTING IS what destroys the yoke. Rituals, a loud voice, a certain way of praying, or any other method will not destroy the yoke of demonic oppression off your life. It is simply and only the anointing that destroys the yoke.

The anointing is the power of God that He places in vessels of His choosing. The anointing is Jesus/the Holy Spirit/the Father, as they are all one. But it is specifically the attribute of Jesus *coming in power.* The power of God is the greatest power in the world. This power can do anything. As children of God, we are given free will, and that includes free will to decide how we will use the anointing. Because of this, God does not give the anointing to everyone. God desires every believer to live a surrendered life that leads to transformation into Christlikeness. When that happens, God deems a person trustworthy of the anointing, and He will pour out the anointing on that person.

Unfortunately, not every believer lives a surrendered life, and therefore not every believer can be trusted with the power of God. There was a reason God chose to anoint David over anyone else. David was surrendered to

God and would steward the anointing and his position according to what God wanted.

> And when He had removed him, He raised up
> David to be their king: of him He testified and said,
> "I have found David the son of Jesse, a man after My
> own heart [conforming to My will and purposes],
> who will do all My will."
>
> —Acts 13:22, amp

Throughout the Word of God, from Old Testament to New Testament, we see God's principles at work, and foremost among them is His principle of healing the sick, casting out demons, and doing all kinds of miracles. The principle of God doing miracles is this: He pours His anointing into a vessel, and He then moves through that vessel to do the miracles. God put His anointing on Moses and moved specifically through Moses to do signs, wonders, and miracles in Egypt that led to the Israelites' deliverance. The sea parted as Moses lifted his staff because he carried the anointing. Joshua was a servant of Moses, the anointed servant of God. Through his surrender and obedience to God and his being a humble and loyal spiritual son of Moses, Joshua received impartation from Moses.

Upon Moses' death Joshua became the anointed leader God moved through to bring the Israelites into the Promised Land. Elijah was anointed by God and did many miracles, including healing the sick and raising the dead as God's power moved through him. Elisha was Elijah's servant and received impartation through Elijah. This impartation included a double portion of anointing that allowed Elisha to do the same kind of miracles Elijah did—and even twice as many!

In the New Testament, Jesus chose and anointed His twelve apostles. And He said, "Whoever believes in me will do the works I have been doing, and they will do even greater things than these" (John 14:12).

> At the hands of the apostles many signs and wonders (attesting miracles) were continually taking place among the people.
>
> —ACTS 5:12, AMP

> A sense of awe was felt by everyone, and many wonders and signs (attesting miracles) were taking place through the apostles.
>
> —ACTS 2:43, AMP

In the Old Testament the anointing found in vessels was rare. But under the new covenant Jesus has sent the Holy Spirit to dwell with all who become believers in Him as Lord. God desires for the Holy Spirit to fill every believer and totally transform the person. When that takes place, the anointing will come. Every believer has the potential to access the anointing, yet it is their decision to make. A life of surrender, humility, and obedience is the only way you can be a chosen one ready to carry the anointing. "For many are called, but few are chosen" (Matt. 22:14, NKJV). Few choose the narrow road that leads to being chosen by God to carry the anointing. Many choose to be lukewarm and lead a more "comfortable" Christian life.

> These signs will accompany those who have believed: in My name they will cast out demons, they will speak in new tongues; they will pick up serpents, and if they drink anything deadly, it will

not hurt them; they will lay hands on the sick, and
they will get well.

—Mark 16:17–18, amp

This is a promise to all who believe! It is not supposed
to be just a handful of ministers who carry the anointing
to cast out demons and heal the sick. The anointing is
for all who believe—meaning true believers who are surrendered to God and obedient to Him. God desires to
be able to move however He wants through you. When
someone is sick, He wants to be able to heal the person
through you. When someone is oppressed, He wants to be
able to cast the demon out through you. When someone
needs to hear His voice, He wants to be able to speak a
prophetic word through you. But because the anointing
could do damage if stewarded wrongly, God goes by His
principles and moves only through a vessel in power if He
sees they can be entrusted with the anointing.

Though God wants to use all believers in power to
heal and deliver, He will pour out His anointing only on
those who are surrendered and obedient to His principles,
including His principles of how to receive the anointing.
Many are under the impression that all believers have the
anointing. If that's the case, why do so many ministers
and believers pray for people yet miracles don't happen,
demons aren't cast out, and the sick aren't healed? The
reason simply is that the anointing is not there!

When a person gives their life to Jesus, they receive
the Holy Spirit to guide, comfort, lead, and transform
them. But there are more indwellings and measures of the
Holy Spirit to receive. The second indwelling is the baptism of the Holy Spirit. This greater measure of the Holy
Spirit is usually poured out on a believer when they have

surrendered and want God to overtake their flesh. The fire of the Holy Spirit and the gift of tongues then help a person live a surrendered life and empower them to witness for Jesus. There is also a third indwelling of the Holy Spirit: the anointing. This measure of the Holy Spirit is not for strengthening one's own spiritual life but purely for ministering to other people. The anointing comes when God can trust you to be selfless, servant-hearted, and ready to do all His will.

When the anointing is truly there, miracles happen with ease! This is what we see in the ministries of Peter and Paul.

> More and more believers in the Lord, crowds of men and women, were constantly being added to their number, to such an extent that they even carried their sick out into the streets and put them on cots and sleeping pads, so that when Peter came by at least his shadow might fall on one of them [with healing power]. And the people from the towns in the vicinity of Jerusalem were coming together, bringing the sick and those who were tormented by unclean spirits, and they were all being healed.
>
> —Acts 5:14–16, AMP

> God was doing extraordinary and unusual miracles by the hands of Paul, so that even handkerchiefs or face-towels or aprons that had touched his skin were brought to the sick, and their diseases left them and the evil spirits came out [of them].
>
> —Acts 19:11–12, AMP

Look at the ease with which people were healed and delivered under Peter's and Paul's ministries! This is what happens when the anointing is present. This is how it's supposed to be today in every church. This is the biblical principle for how to seek and find deliverance and healing from Jesus: find the anointing and go where the anointing is. Position yourself under the "shadow" of the anointing.

The anointing was being released through Peter as he ministered, and the Scripture says that *all* who came to receive what he was releasing received! The anointing coming out of Peter was like a waterfall. All the people had to do was position themselves under the waterfall and they got drenched. No demon or sickness could stay. No "dryness" or death could stay in their bodies. The kingdom of heaven came on them as they simply did things God's way and followed His principle of receiving healing and deliverance.

WHAT MAKES DEMONS GO

When a child of God commands demons to go according to the principles, or laws, of the spiritual realm that God has established in His kingdom, the demons are forced to leave.

> If anyone competes as an athlete [in competitive games], he is not crowned [with the wreath of victory] unless he competes according to the rules.
> —2 TIMOTHY 2:5, AMP

For athletes to be allowed to compete for the top prize, they must follow the stated rules of the competition and meet the qualification standards. Athletes are given the opportunity to compete and may ultimately be given the chance to claim victory once they follow the specific rules of competition. Just as athletes must follow the rules of competition, believers must learn and follow the principles that rule the spiritual realm.

Demons know the spiritual laws perfectly because they are spirits and therefore see spiritually. Many believers are blind to the laws of the spiritual realm, and that is why they are unsuccessful in casting out demons. Demons don't have to obey if a child of God is operating outside the laws of the spiritual realm. It's as if the believer is disqualified from casting out the demons because they broke the rules. As you continue to read, you will discover the spiritual laws that must be understood and followed to successfully cast out demons.

Here are the three keys that, when used correctly, ensure demons must go:

1. Receive true authority from Christ.

> The seventy returned with joy, saying, "Lord, even the demons are subject to us in Your name." He said to them, "I watched Satan fall from heaven like [a flash of] lightning. Listen carefully: I have given you authority [that you now possess] to tread on serpents and scorpions, and [the ability to exercise authority] over all the power of the enemy (Satan); and nothing will [in any way] harm you."
> —Luke 10:17–19, amp

Jesus sent seventy of His disciples out to minister to people and also gave them the power to cast out demons. The demons obeyed the disciples and left the people being ministered to. Jesus then explained that the demons obeyed the disciples because He had given the disciples authority over them. When Jesus gives authority, it also means He gives anointing. Authority and anointing come together—when there is anointing, there is also authority, and vice versa.

The president of a country is given authority over situations, people, weapons, and armies that they did not have prior to taking that position. The president is also given power to enforce their authority. For example, a president is given the power of the military, police, and government to enforce whatever he or she authorizes. When God is ready to pour out His anointing on you, He gives you His power and authority. He gives you authority over demons, and He gives you His power to enforce the authority you have. Even if the demons try to delay and fight the command you've given, the power of God will come on them like fire and force them to go. When God gives a person authority, the demons truly recognize that authority.

> A group of Jews was traveling from town to town casting out evil spirits. They tried to use the name of the Lord Jesus in their incantation, saying, "I command you in the name of Jesus, whom Paul preaches, to come out!" Seven sons of Sceva, a leading priest, were doing this. But one time when they tried it, the evil spirit replied, "I know Jesus, and I know Paul, but who are you?"
> —Acts 19:13–15, NLT

What the evil spirit was really saying was this: "I know that Jesus and Paul have authority over me, and I'm forced to obey their commands because of the spiritual laws. But I see spiritually that you don't have this same authority that Jesus and Paul have over us, so therefore I will not obey you."

Receiving authority over demons comes when God deems

you trustworthy to receive the anointing and authority. It comes after surrendering to God, being tested through refining fire (again and again), and continually being obedient. It also comes in God's perfect timing, which sometimes can be years after you originally surrender to God. Moreover, God may release a small portion of anointing early on in your surrender to see how you steward it. Just because you see anointing moving through you, do not take it to mean God automatically deems you completely trustworthy. Many times, He pours a measure of anointing on a person as a test, not as a stamp of approval.

2. Have confident faith in the authority you carry.

Jesus has given the free gift of salvation to every person on this earth. Yet only those who believe that Jesus is Lord will receive salvation. Jesus has paid the price for every child of God to be healed and set free. Yet only those who believe that this gift of healing and freedom is theirs will receive it. This principle of faith applies to everything in the kingdom of God. You access the kingdom by faith. You access the ability to cast out demons by faith too. If you don't have faith in the authority God has given you, that authority you have will not work for you.

God may give you anointing and authority to cast out demons, but what will you do when a demon starts speaking lies through a person and tries to intimidate you? Will you believe you truly have the anointing and authority to cast the demon out? The authority you have works only when you believe you truly have it. A schoolteacher is given a position of authority over students. But if the teacher doesn't have the confidence to stand strong and discipline the students when they act up, the authority won't work. The children will walk all over the teacher.

Demons come from the devil, who is the father of lies. Therefore, demons lie. They don't want to be cast out, so often they will lie to you, saying, "You don't have authority over me," or "I will not go," or "She/he is mine." The demons' aim is to get you to believe their lies so you will back down and stop asserting your authority over them.

When I was new in the ministry of deliverance, in my fourth month of casting out demons, I was ministering at one of our first revival events. So many demons were leaving people all over the church as God's power moved mightily. All of a sudden, a demon aggressively yelled through a man, "I don't like you up there! What do you got to say about me?" This demon was trying to intimidate me. It spoke through the man as if the man were a huge boxer trying to challenge me to a fight that he would obviously win because of his size. (He was over six feet tall and muscular.) I could tell the ushers were genuinely concerned about my safety.

By the grace of God, I had been discipled by my spiritual father, Prophet Dr. GeorDavie, who is a giant in the spirit and a general in the kingdom of God. Under his mentorship God had prepared me to be strong, courageous, and unwavering in faith that greater is He who is in me than he who is in the world (1 John 4:4). So I looked into the man's eyes and said boldly, "Come here." The demon overtook the man at that point, so when I told the demon to come, it had to obey and walk to the altar. The man walked aggressively toward me and started yelling at me with an intimidating, angry voice. I stood my ground and calmly yet firmly said, "I break every curse off of this man now."

The demon then said through the man fiercely, "I wish you'd shut up right now!"

I said, "I will not shut up. I must command you to leave, because this man belongs to Jesus."

At one point the demon said, "It ain't gonna happen, lady."

As I stood firm in the truth, knowing the demon was a liar, I used the keys of the kingdom (including asking the man to renounce open doors that had led to the oppression, which you'll learn about in a later chapter) and commanded the demon to leave, and the demon left the man!

If I had looked at the physical reality—a big man yelling in a strong and intimidating way toward me—rather than the spiritual reality, I would've given in to fear. But by God's grace I stayed focused on the spiritual truths and kept believing in the authority I carried. The demons had no choice but to obey since I kept my faith in Jesus, who was with me.

As I've ministered through the years, there have been many situations just like this—a demon screaming through a person, "I will not leave!" Some demons have responded adamantly "No!" when I first start commanding curses to be broken. At other times a demon has overtaken the person, and they started to run out of the revival tent or toward the back of the church. In these cases, just as a parent would say "Sit down!" or "Come back here!" if their child walked away from them in disobedience and disrespect, I spoke with authority, "Come back here now!" Each time this happened, as tough as the demon first appeared to be, they were forced to obey the command, and the person (with the demon overtaking them) came toward me. I then commanded the demon to go, and it had to leave.

When a person receives deliverance, you'll usually see them go from one extreme to another. At first the demon overtakes them, filling them with immense rage. Then, once the demon has to leave, the person immediately comes to, starts weeping, and is filled with childlike joy and awe of Jesus!

3. Execute your authority properly.

A leader can know they have authority, but they still must execute their authority properly. Imagine a classroom where most of the students are misbehaving. Some are being loud, some are fighting, and others are running around the classroom. The teacher has been given authority over the students but must understand the principles of authority and adequately execute that authority by sternly telling the students to stop at once. A disciplinary action may be required to bring order.

To show an example of a wrong way to execute authority over the students, imagine the teacher thinks that one stern command for all the students isn't enough. Instead, they request that several other teachers enter the classroom and then assigns each student to a one-on-one meeting with another teacher, and the teachers each repeat the same stern command. The original teacher would not be operating in the true principle of authority. They would not be realizing the way authority works and that they had been given authority over all the children. All the teacher has to do is believe it and walk in their authority.

In the spiritual realm the same principles of authority apply. Let's revisit a passage we considered earlier in this chapter to see a biblical example of walking in authority properly:

> They even carried their sick out into the streets and put them on cots and sleeping pads, so that when Peter came by at least his shadow might fall on one of them

[with healing power]. And the people from the towns in the vicinity of Jerusalem were coming together, bringing the sick and those who were tormented by unclean spirits, and they were all being healed.

—Acts 5:15–16, amp

Each place Peter ministered, whether in a temple or church or an outside area, was considered his spiritual territory where he had complete authority. Demons have to leave when authority is executed. So, whether one demon is present in a crowd of one thousand people or five thousand demons are present in a crowd of one thousand people (many demons per person), all demons have to leave when true authority is properly executed over them.

The reason why *all* who came under the shadow of Peter were delivered and healed was that (1) Peter carried true, high-level authority, where even principalities had to obey, and (2) Peter executed his authority properly. He didn't get intimidated by the crowd. He didn't limit God and think "I must pray for each person individually." He understood how authority works. He was confident in the anointing and authority he carried. He also knew that as he just spoke the command, all demons and illnesses had to go from every person who was positioned to receive the anointing through him. He didn't assign other ministers to help him cast out demons and heal the sick, because that would have meant operating outside the laws of authority, just as a mayor doesn't send out teams to knock on every resident's door to repeat words he has already spoken for all.

We are all called to walk in authority but never outside our individual spiritual territory. A mayor in one city has their own territory, and a mayor in another city has a different territory. The mayors execute authority in their own domains; they don't have the same authority in other people's territories.

The Roman centurion who came to Jesus understood how authority works and therefore was able to see God do a miracle for his servant.

> As Jesus went into Capernaum, a centurion came up to Him, begging Him [for help], and saying, "Lord, my servant is lying at home paralyzed, with intense and terrible, tormenting pain." Jesus said to him, "I will come and heal him." But the centurion replied to Him, "Lord, I am not worthy to have You come under my roof, but only say the word, and my servant will be healed. For I also am a man subject to authority [of a higher rank], with soldiers subject to me; and I say to one, 'Go!' and he goes, and to another, 'Come!' and he comes, and to my slave, 'Do this!' and he does it." When Jesus heard this, He was amazed and said to those who were following Him, "I tell you truthfully, I have not found such great faith [as this] with anyone in Israel."... Then Jesus said to the centurion, "Go; it will be done for you as you have believed." And the servant was restored to health at that very hour.
>
> —MATTHEW 8:5–10, 13, AMP

Jesus offered to come in person and pray for the servant individually. But the centurion understood how authority worked in his day-to-day routine as a soldier and had faith that the same principles of authority also applied to the spiritual realm. He understood that it wasn't a one-on-one prayer that makes demons and sickness go. Demons go when an anointed vessel executes their authority, even when they do so from a distance or to the back of a crowd. The centurion's greater revelation and greater faith blessed Jesus, because Jesus knew more miracles can take place with this kind of faith—faith that takes the limits off God and allows Him to do so much more.

I have seen God move in this limitless, powerful way as I minister to crowds. When I declare, "This spirit of infirmity must go!" several people fall down as the power of God hits them and delivers them. At the same moment, some shriek loudly (Acts 8:7) and others cough as demons leave them. Still others have no manifestation but are indeed set free, as they testify later.

When I minister online, mass deliverance just like what I described happens. Sometimes we can actually see it on a Zoom call—people falling back, others coughing, others weeping, while still others have no manifestations but are set free. Live comments will flood the feed, with many people testifying of how they felt the demons leave them. Others testify of being set free and healed without a one-on-one prayer. They simply positioned themselves under the "shadow of anointing," and the execution of authority was effective. The demons and illnesses had to go!

I recently ministered in an arena in Manila, Philippines, where eight thousand people were gathered. When I declared that demonic spirits must go, you could suddenly hear demons shrieking as they left people all over the arena. I saw people falling down under the power of God everywhere. So many testified that they were delivered and healed, all the way at the back of the arena. God delivered thousands of people at one time as I executed my authority and released the anointing.

The way Jesus and Peter cast out demons and healed the sick is the proper way to execute authority, leading to the most effective deliverance and healing. Operating in line with God's spiritual laws includes executing authority properly. If you're not executing your authority properly, technically you're not in line with God's principles. When you operate outside God's principles, demons can hide and fool around. It's just like when a teacher doesn't execute their authority properly; the students know it and will take advantage, fooling around.

The same goes for the spiritual realm. The main reason ministers and believers in general struggle to cast out demons is that (1) they lack the anointing/authority or (2) they *do not execute their authority properly*. What I've shared in this section is one of the huge keys of the kingdom that God has led me to release in this book, and I believe it's also one of the reasons why there is effectiveness and the real fruits of deliverance and healing in my ministry—glory to God!

UNDERSTANDING SPIRITUAL TERRITORIES

A principle of authority is that one who has authority has a specific territory or dominion where their authority is effective. Just as a president only has dominion over their nation, we too have a specific spiritual territory where our authority operates. The spiritual territory of a fivefold leader includes everyone who attends their church. The spiritual territory of a believer who attends that church may include family and friends, coworkers, or people they meet while running errands or traveling—anyone God leads them to minister to (outside the church congregants) who is open to hear about Jesus or receive prayer.

Here's one example of ministering deliverance properly in your domain. At your workplace during lunch, a coworker opens up to you after you have shone your light (of Jesus) daily and been loving to them. The coworker tells you they struggle with depression. They notice that you always seem to be joyful, even when going through hard times. The coworker asks what your secret is. This is an indication that the person is open and giving you their free will to share about God.

This person has just stepped inside your spiritual territory. You tell them your joy is because of Jesus and then share your testimony, letting them know that deliverance is possible through Jesus. The coworker says they want freedom from depression. You then can ask if they'd like you to pray for them because you believe Jesus wants to free them right now. If they say yes, you can execute your authority and command the spirit of depression to leave.

The church is supposed to be a place where you receive equipping and impartation to walk in your authority in your own domain. It is not supposed to be a place where several people try to assist "Peter" (the pastor) in casting out demons. The authority and anointing are more than enough in a true anointed leader. We are not just believers who attend church. We are part of God's *kingdom*. A kingdom is a type of government, and the kingdom of God includes the government of the spiritual realm that we are also a part of. In any government different leaders are appointed with different levels of authority to accomplish the vision of the nation.

America has a vision to bring peace, freedom, justice, prosperity, and opportunity to all people in the nation. This is accomplished by individuals walking in authority in their own positions in society, such as the president, governors, mayors, lawyers, judges, police officers, teachers, doctors, business owners, and parents (who have authority over their children). All these examples have their own territories where they execute authority to do their jobs and bring about the vision.

This is how it is in the kingdom of God. Jesus is the King of His kingdom. He appoints and anoints fivefold ministers to be in places of high-level authority, just as people are appointed within governments and earthly kingdoms. He has appointed every child of God to operate in various levels and positions of authority. When we all execute our authority in our own territories, God's kingdom vision is accomplished. God's vision for the kingdom we are a part of is to destroy the devil's works and advance His kingdom: to open blind eyes to God's love, bring healing to the sick, and set free the oppressed.

If parents try to go into a classroom and do the teacher's job, there will be problems. It will bring disorder and disrupt what is supposed to be achieved.

> Jesus knew their thoughts and said to them, "Every kingdom divided against itself will be ruined, and every city or household divided against itself will not stand."
>
> —MATTHEW 12:25

If the kingdom of God is divided regarding God's principle of authority, there will be loopholes for demons. We will be most effective in destroying the devil's kingdom when we are united. Also, the more obedient you are to God, doing things His way and executing your authority adequately, the more anointing and authority He will give you, and the more demons will respect you. Earlier, we noted how demons respected Paul. It was clear to them that he was truly anointed, had high-level authority, and was walking in his authority adequately. These factors made them automatically respect him and be unable to fool around when he commanded them to go.

For you to receive deliverance, it's important to know how deliverance actually works. The most important key to receiving deliverance is positioning yourself where the anointing is being released, just as people did in the apostle Peter's day. It is also critical that you position yourself under a truly anointed ministry where authority is executed properly. Do not go to just any deliverance minister. Some are operating without the revelation of the principle of authority I've shared in this chapter.

When seeking an anointed ministry to position yourself under, it's vital to determine that this new-wine revelation of how to adequately cast out demons is operating there. It's not supposed to take several hours and be very painful when receiving deliverance. You're not supposed to be manhandled, and the minister should not have to struggle so much to cast out the demon. Demonic oppression will leave you with ease as you position yourself where true, high-level anointing and authority are flowing through a servant of God. That anointing and authority are moving through these pages! You will receive deliverance as you keep reading—and receive it with ease!

If you're looking for a church to attend either in person or online, I recommend 5F Church (my church). You will encounter the power of God and receive the miracles you need as you position yourself there.

Chapter 5

WHAT MAKES DEMONS GO—KEY 2: FAITH

U P TO THIS point I have explained how demonic oppression happens and that the most important key to unlocking your deliverance is anointing. We also discussed the importance of positioning yourself where the anointing is released. Now it's time to learn that *faith* is another vital key to deliverance.

Everything in the kingdom of God is received by grace, through faith (Eph. 2:8). This is the way to receive not only revelation in the spiritual realm but also healing and deliverance. Many people are not accessing their full inheritance as children of God simply because they don't have faith that it's theirs. Many believers accept only God's salvation that frees them from an eternity in hell because that is all they are believing for. But the more we believe in, the more we will receive. Jesus has promised us abundant life. To receive this abundant life, we must believe abundantly. We must believe that He will provide this life He has promised.

Do you know what faith really is? You may have a partial understanding, but in this chapter I'm going to reveal how to have true faith. When you understand and apply all the aspects of faith, any miracle is possible. Nothing will be able to stop you from receiving deliverance.

FAITH THAT HEALING AND FREEDOM ARE YOURS

The first aspect of faith you must have is the belief that healing and freedom are a part of your inheritance as a child of God. "By His stripes we are healed" (Isa. 53:5, NKJV) means that Jesus endured scourging. This scourging created wounds that looked like stripes on His back, causing His precious blood to be shed. This blood was not shed for nothing! God allowed Jesus to endure this torture for a purpose: to pay the price and make the sacrifice for you to receive healing and freedom from the devil's grip. Deliverance is the children's bread (Mark 7:27). In other words those who come to Jesus with childlike hearts of faith *will* receive freedom.

As soon as you give your life to Jesus, you receive an inheritance from God as His child, and this inheritance includes healing and freedom. The works of the devil in your life that have brought sickness and oppression must be gone! It's as if it's written in a contract in the spiritual realm. An earthly inheritance is made up of possessions. If anyone tries to steal the house, money, or jewelry you inherited, they will be stopped. Legally these possessions are *yours*. Nobody can change that!

This is exactly how it is in the spiritual realm. So often people beg God for healing and deliverance as if these aren't their inheritance. They pray as if these are things God has yet to give them. But technically God has already given you healing and freedom. He wants you to believe that they're yours. It is important you have this kind of faith. Knowing your identity and rights as a child of God is a crucial part of accessing your healing and deliverance. Walking in your authority and rejecting the devil's lie that "sickness and oppression are your portion" are vital in accessing your healing and freedom. Having the mindset of "I guess Jesus doesn't want to heal me; it hasn't happened yet, and I've prayed so much" is not faith. Having faith that *healing and deliverance are your inheritance* is how you access the miracles!

Think of it as though Jesus has prepared Christmas gifts for you. They were very expensive. They're wrapped up, and they have your name on them. Jesus has handed the gifts to you. They're yours! But you have to open the gifts to actually receive them and use them. Faith is how you unwrap the gifts. You don't need to ask Jesus to go get you gifts. He's already presented them to you. Now you need to unwrap them by having faith that they're truly yours. Be like a child, who is quick to unwrap a gift as soon as they see their name on it.

If you come to a church or ministry event where the power of God is moving, you may witness some people receiving miracles while others are not. The main reason people don't receive their miracles is that they don't have the necessary faith that Jesus indeed wants to heal and deliver them. Many do not have the accurate faith that Jesus has paid the price for their healing, so therefore the miracle is going to take place. This is why the revelation of what having faith means is so important.

Many people believe in God and His goodness, but they just stop there in terms of faith. They act robotically, thinking, "Well, if God wants to heal me, He will, and if He doesn't, He won't." That's like a child saying, "If my parents want me to have this present, they will unwrap it for me." We have to do our part when it comes to faith that God wants to heal and deliver us. Jesus has done His part and already paid the price for our healing, our miracles. We can't be robots and just do nothing. We need to have faith!

> A woman in the crowd had suffered for twelve years with constant bleeding. She had suffered a great deal from many doctors, and over the years she had spent everything she had to pay them, but she had gotten no better. In fact, she had gotten worse. She had heard about Jesus, so she came up behind him through the crowd and touched his robe. For she thought to herself, "If I can just touch his robe, I will be healed." Immediately the bleeding stopped, and she could feel in her body that she had been healed of her terrible condition.
>
> Jesus realized at once that healing power had gone out from him, so he turned around in the crowd and asked, "Who touched my robe?"
>
> His disciples said to him, "Look at this crowd pressing around you. How can you ask, 'Who touched me?'"
>
> But he kept on looking around to see who had done it. Then the frightened woman, trembling at the realization of what had happened to her, came and fell to her knees in front of him and told him what she had done. And he said to her, "Daughter, your faith has made you well. Go in peace. Your suffering is over."
>
> —MARK 5:25–34, NLT

This woman "heard about Jesus." She had heard the testimonies that Jesus was healing all who came to Him. She then believed "Jesus wants to heal me." Her faith wasn't simply "I believe that Jesus is Lord, and if He wants to heal me, He will. But I'm not sure." She had this confidence that when she came into His presence, she *would* be healed: "If I can just touch His robe, I *will* be healed."

Notice she said *will*, not maybe. Jesus did not call her selfish, pushy, or prideful for confidently grabbing her healing. Jesus called it faith. He revealed that because she had this true faith, she was able to receive her healing. Look at the power of faith! This woman came with faith, positioned herself where the anointing was flowing, and immediately was healed. The power of God located her because of her faith. Her faith attracted the power of God to touch her. Jesus did not turn to her and say, "Be healed." Just positioning herself where the anointing was flowing immediately released healing to her!

FAITH IN GOD'S WAY OF HEALING AND DELIVERING

In addition to having faith that healing and freedom are your inheritance, there is another aspect of faith you must have, in most cases, to receive your miracle. When God releases healing, deliverance, and miracles, He chooses to move in power through His anointed vessels.

For various reasons some people are uncomfortable with God's method of moving in power through human vessels. Some have experienced church hurt and seen abuses of power. Out of fear they feel uncomfortable witnessing a servant of God operating in divine power. But just because we have seen abuses of power in various churches doesn't mean we should throw out God's method of releasing miracles. Just because there have been corrupt ministers doesn't mean all ministers are corrupt.

Some people are jealous of servants of God who walk

in the anointing and are elevated for God's glory. Many wrongly believe that there are no longer any apostles today and that all prophets are fake. According to Ephesians 4:11–16, Christ gave apostles, prophets, evangelists, pastors, and teachers to the body as gifts for equipping, maturing, and imparting so that these offices will continue until Jesus returns.

> [He did this] to fully equip and perfect the saints (God's people) for works of service, to build up the body of Christ [the church]; *until we all reach oneness in the faith and in the knowledge of the Son of God, [growing spiritually] to become a mature believer, reaching to the measure of the fullness of Christ* [manifesting His spiritual completeness and exercising our spiritual gifts in unity].
> —EPHESIANS 4:12–13, AMP, EMPHASIS ADDED

Other people who are uncomfortable with God's way of moving in power are married to tradition. They are unwilling to accept a new move of God where the Holy Spirit is doing something we haven't seen in recent times. By and large, the body of Christ hasn't seen modern-day Peters and Pauls. By and large, they haven't seen servants of God operating in the anointing as the fivefold ministers did in the Book of Acts.

Too many people are quick to discount a new way God is moving simply because it's new and unique. Some people consider anything different to be wrong just because it's different. Yet God calls us to follow His Word rather than present-day Christian culture and traditions. And the truth is, *there is nothing new about the power of God moving through anointed vessels!* The Book of Acts is our blueprint for what the church is supposed to look like, where signs and wonders "follow them that believe" (Mark 16:17, kjv) in a constant flow, a constant demonstration that the kingdom of God has invaded the earth!

God is now raising up and anointing modern-day Peters and Pauls. He is moving today just as He did through those two apostles. The sick and demon-oppressed are coming by the masses to where the anointing is being released, under true anointed apostles and prophets. The anointing is moving with ease, casting out demon after demon and healing all different kinds of sicknesses and diseases. There are no struggles with demons. The anointing is true and so powerful that demons flee at just one command—and in some cases as soon as the person walks in the church.

The people don't have to be manhandled, be pushed down, or have strange techniques applied to them (e.g., placing objects on them) for the demons to leave. Simply by the authority executed in word, the demons flee.

The anointed healings and deliverances I've described happen at the church I pastor, 5F Church, and at the events and conferences where I minister. All glory to God! I'm absolutely in awe that by His grace He would release His precious anointing on my life and use me as a vessel. I never wanted to be a minister. I never wanted to be a leader, and I definitely couldn't picture it. I never wanted to speak in front of people because it was my biggest fear and weakness. And although seeing people encounter God's love through His power was my greatest joy, I had no desire to cast out demons. (I had seen only a couple of people cast out demons before.)

Nonetheless, God called me to be an apostle. I remember Mary's response to God's calling when she said to the angel, "I am the Lord's servant....May your word to me be fulfilled" (Luke 1:38). That's what I said in my heart as I accepted the call. I'm so humbled that God uses me to deliver and help His people. I'm so grateful for His mighty anointing that He has released to the body of Christ in this hour that has caused revival to break out.

> Believe in the LORD your God, and you shall be established; believe His prophets, and you shall prosper.
>
> —2 CHRONICLES 20:20, NKJV

I've experienced the truth of this scripture in my life. As I have believed and trusted my spiritual father, who is a prophet, I have succeeded and prospered in my calling. As I have followed his prophetic direction and believed the words declared over me, I have experienced freedom, healing, and abundance in every area of my life.

To prosper in health and every other area of life, you need to believe the true servants of God. Recognize and honor the true apostles and prophets of today, in addition to the other fivefold offices. You will know them by their fruit:

> You can identify them by their fruit, that is, by the way they act. Can you pick grapes from thornbushes, or figs from thistles? A good tree produces good fruit, and a bad tree produces bad fruit. A good tree can't produce bad fruit, and a bad tree can't produce good fruit.
>
> —MATTHEW 7:16–18, NLT

God calls us to look for the good fruit, and when we find it, we can know it's a good tree: a true anointed servant of God. As God helps you see who is true, you are then called to trust and believe. You are called to come humbly to the church or event where an anointed servant of God is ministering. Come with faith, believing that there is true anointing on this servant of God and that the anointing will come on you to heal and deliver you. The Scripture says that *all* were healed under the apostle Peter's shadow (of anointing).

One of the secrets of why all were healed is that the people had trust and faith in Peter's ministry. They had heard the testimonies and seen the fruit. They trusted and believed in God's way of releasing miracles through His anointed servants. The people had no doubt or skepticism about Peter's ministry. They had faith both in Peter's anointing and in God's ways of moving through him. They had understanding and faith in how authority works, just as the Roman centurion exhibited when he asked Jesus to "only say the word" (Matt. 8:8).

Some people today may believe that a servant of God is anointed, but they don't have faith in God's way of moving through that servant of God. Many people have faith in one-on-one prayer and traditional ways of praying. But having faith in these alone isn't really having faith in God to heal you; rather, it's putting faith in a person to heal you. If that is your thinking, your faith isn't "adding up" in the spiritual realm, and you can miss your miracle. Miracles happen when there is true faith in God and His ways of moving in power through anointed vessels walking in their God-given authority/anointing.

To demonstrate your faith in God's way of releasing miracles, position yourself where the anointing is flowing, either by attending church or a ministry event in person or by watching online. Come with faith that since you are following God's principle of how to receive healing and deliverance, you *will* receive them! You simply come in confidence, knowing that just as *all* were healed under Peter's shadow, you will be healed today. God *will* move in power on you however He wants, whether via a one-on-one prayer with the anointed servant of God or by the word being declared. You come with faith, knowing that every demon and sickness has to go because of God's system of using anointed servants to execute their authority.

Not all miracles manifest immediately, but God's Word never returns void (Isa. 55:11, NKJV). Elijah's servant did not see the rain cloud immediately after the prophet first told him to look for it, but it didn't mean the miracle wasn't happening. Elijah kept telling his servant to go back and look for the cloud. Sure enough, the seventh time, the rain cloud appeared (1 Kings 18:43–44). Why didn't the rain cloud appear the first time?

Likewise, Elisha told Naaman to dip himself in the water seven times. On the seventh time he was healed of leprosy (2 Kings 5:10–15). Why seven times? Why couldn't the healing happen after the first time?

Jesus told ten lepers to go show themselves to the priests. On their way there, they were healed (Luke 17:12–14). Why didn't their leprosy disappear immediately? Why did it take time for them to be healed?

The simple answer to all these questions is that God chooses to release healing and deliverance in this way sometimes. He chooses to begin the healing in the spiritual realm and work in a person's life—like spiritual surgery—until they start to see and feel the result of what has already taken place in the spirit. Sometimes He does this for no specific reason. He just chooses to do it this way. Other times the waiting process is a test of faith, obedience, and humility.

God uses various circumstances to test us and refine us. For some, waiting for the healing to manifest is where He purposely brings the testing. When you see a person delivered immediately yet you don't see any difference in yourself, it doesn't mean God loves the other person more. It doesn't necessarily mean the other person has more faith than you. Many times it means God is purposefully choosing to heal and deliver you over time, in a process, for His perfect purposes.

When you receive a declaration from an anointed vessel of God such as "All demonic spirits must go; all sickness must go," it is vital that you *believe* these words will not return void. In fact, believe that the miracle has taken place the moment the word was declared, whether one-on-one or corporately. That is the action of receiving your miracle. It's like the servant of God is throwing a ball. If your hands are not up and open, the ball will go right past you. However, if your hands are up, you will catch the ball. Believing and confessing "I receive; I am healed; I am free; I believe I just received my miracle" is the action of lifting your hands and catching the ball.

As you leave the gathering, it's important that you keep declaring and believing that you are healed and free and that the miracle *will* manifest to the physical realm. This is the action of continuing to go look for the cloud, to keep dipping yourself in the water, to walk in obedience to "show [yourself] to the priests."

Do not drop the ball! Do not claim "I receive" in the church service and then the next day, once you haven't seen the miracle manifest yet, drop the ball by thinking, "I guess I wasn't healed." Don't let the devil's lies cause you to drop your miracle! Don't cut the spiritual surgery short before the surgeon has finished. You need to get serious in the spiritual realm and fight for your miracles! So many are aborting their miracles because they have not been equipped with this spiritual knowledge. I urge you to take these words seriously. God doesn't want you to miss out on the miracles He releases ever again.

When all these aspects of faith are present, I believe we will see the Book of Acts come alive, and it will be exactly how it was with Peter's shadow. *All* were healed. Your faith will grow as you continue to believe that God wants to heal and free you. Remember to trust that God's ways of healing and deliverance are perfect. No matter your past, no matter your thoughts, Jesus' love for you remains the same.

Chapter 6

HOW TO ACTIVATE FAITH

THE MOST COMMON misconception about faith is that it is based on feeling. The truth is that faith is a choice. God reveals His love to you, and you become aware that His existence is undeniable. You can't see Him physically or prove Him scientifically, but deep down you know He's real. It's up to you to choose to believe He is Lord. If you're someone who must have proof and loves logic, you will be tempted with thoughts and feelings that go against the belief that God is real and that He is Lord. You must make the choice to resist the doubting thoughts.

When you first gave your life to Jesus, you probably had strong feelings of faith. But that doesn't mean feelings always have to be there. Real faith is enduring. Real faith is making the choice to submit your thoughts and feelings to the covenant you made with God the day you decided to follow Him. Real faith is choosing to believe the Word of God when your feelings don't align with God's truth. Faith is about obedience—obedience in taking God's Word as truth.

> For just as the [human] body without the spirit is dead,
> so faith without works [of obedience] is also dead.
> —JAMES 2:26, AMP

The scripture doesn't say "faith without feelings" is dead. It says "faith without works" is dead. Faith is an action, a choice to take what God says in His Word as truth. Faith is being like a child who just takes whatever their parent says as truth. The child doesn't need evidence. The child doesn't take time to question what the parent says. The child doesn't believe only if their feelings match up with their belief. The child simply believes.

> At that time the disciples came to Jesus and asked, "Who, then, is the greatest in the kingdom of heaven?"
> He called a little child to him, and placed the child among them. And he said: "Truly I tell you, unless you change and become like little children, you will never enter the kingdom of heaven."
> —MATTHEW 18:1–3

One of the ways to "become like little children" is to have childlike faith. In the Gospels, when Jesus says things like "Your faith has made you well," this is the faith He is talking about. In speaking to Jairus after his daughter had died, Jesus revealed a key that would release the miracle of resurrection: just believe!

> While Jesus was still speaking, someone came from the house of Jairus, the synagogue leader. "Your daughter is dead," he said. "Don't bother the teacher anymore."
> Hearing this, Jesus said to Jairus, "Don't be afraid; just believe, and she will be healed."
> —LUKE 8:49–50

Many times after Jesus healed or delivered a person, He shared with them why this miracle took place: because they believed!

"What do you want me to do for you?" Jesus asked him.

The blind man said, "Rabbi, I want to see."

"Go," said Jesus, "your faith has healed you." Immediately he received his sight and followed Jesus along the road.

—Mark 10:51–52

Then he touched their eyes and said, "According to your faith let it be done to you"; and their sight was restored.

—Matthew 9:29–30

The Scripture says *according to* their faith," which means because of their faith the miracles could happen.

Then he said to him, "Rise and go; your faith has made you well."

—Luke 17:19

God measures faith by your words and actions, not your feelings. With this revelation nothing can stop you from having huge faith. Without this revelation you would always have a wishy-washy, up-and-down faith; on the mountaintops you would have faith, but in the valleys you would doubt. The spiritual war we are in is centered mostly in the mind. The mind is where our thoughts and feelings are. If you've ever had an unwelcome thought intrude into your mind, that was not your thought. It was the devil's ammunition. He was hoping you would be tricked into thinking it was your own original thought and therefore would believe the thought was the truth. From there you would then act out that truth and live in it. This is the enemy's main strategy against every person.

By getting you to believe his lies, he's actually granted authority by you and therefore can dictate your life.

By saying, "Take captive every thought to make it obedient to Christ" (2 Cor. 10:5), the Bible is telling you that you will have thoughts that are not your own but are from the enemy. That includes thoughts of doubt such as "I don't think I will be healed" and "I don't know if God really wants to heal me." You don't have to accept those thoughts as your own. When you accept Jesus as Lord, you accept Him in all His ways. His main way of speaking is through His Word. Jesus is the embodiment of the Word:[1] "In the beginning was the Word, and the Word was with God, and the Word was God" (John 1:1). When you choose to make Jesus your Lord, you're also choosing to make the Word your truth. In the Word it says that by His stripes you are healed. It also says that you have an inheritance from God and that "the thief comes only in order to steal and kill and destroy. I came that they may have and enjoy life, and have it in abundance [to the full, till it overflows]" (John 10:10, AMP).

These scriptures are now your truth, no matter how you feel about them on any given day. Your choice is more powerful than your feelings. You have authority over your feelings. Your feelings must submit to your authority. David demonstrated this spiritual principle when he was in a valley season, experiencing so much spiritual attack.

> So then, my soul, why would you be depressed? Why would you sink into despair? Just keep hoping and waiting on God, your Savior. For no matter what, I will still sing with praise, for you are my saving grace!
>
> —Psalm 42:5, TPT

David was waiting and waiting for God to defend him and bring him victory. In this scripture he admitted he was having feelings of depression and despair. As days passed and the attacks became more severe, he faced a temptation to give in to those feelings. But he knew that his feelings were not in line with the truth he chose to believe: the Word of God and the character of God. So he took authority over his soul and spoke. When David says, "No matter what," he is making a choice! No matter how he felt, he was making the choice to always keep believing.

God does not make it difficult to have faith. You don't have to wait for the feelings to come. You don't have to wait for the devil to stop attacking your mind. You can use the authority God has given you and take action now! You can reject the devil's lies and choose God's truth by speaking it aloud. Your confession is what God counts as faith. You can have many thoughts that you won't be healed, but God is not looking at your feelings. He's listening to what you speak.

When you declare, "I am healed by Jesus' stripes" and "I know Jesus wants to heal me, for this is my inheritance," God counts this as your faith. Faith is when you speak, "I believe in God's ways of moving through anointed vessels. I believe that the anointing moving through this vessel is true and that healing/deliverance will come as I position myself under the anointing." Your faith and declaration are what release the power of God to heal and deliver you.

CAN SOMEONE BE HEALED WITHOUT FAITH?

In most cases the main keys needed to unlock healing and deliverance are the anointing (positioning yourself where it is being released) and faith. However, this does not mean that a person's faith is always required for their deliverance and healing to take place.

For instance, the Bible records instances where a master's, a parent's, and some friends' faith released the miracles. A Roman centurion had faith for his servant to be healed. Jesus said, "'Go back home. Because you believed, it has happened.' And the young servant was healed that same hour" (Matt. 8:13, NLT).

Jesus said to Jairus, "Just have faith, and [your daughter] will be healed" (Luke 8:50, NLT). When Jairus believed and Jesus commanded the girl to "get up" (v. 54), she rose from the dead.

On another occasion a few men carried a paralyzed man on a sleeping mat and lowered him down through a roof into the crowd, in front of Jesus. "Seeing their faith, Jesus said to the man, 'Young man, your sins are forgiven'" (Luke 5:20, NLT). Seeing *their* faith, not the man's own faith, is what led Jesus to heal the man.

In all these cases it was a person or people believing for a loved one that released the miracle. Today Jesus moves in this same way—sometimes a person receives healing and deliverance because of another's faith. One time at my church, as I began praying for a family, the teenage child started to manifest. Then demons left him, and he fell to the ground. Once he got up, he took off his glasses and with an awestruck expression declared, "I can see!"

His mom shared later that he was depressed and just stayed in his room all the time. He didn't want to go to church that day, but his mom insisted. So, he didn't come with faith, but his mom did, and Jesus moved on her faith! The young man shared a testimony after the service explaining that once he was delivered, as he lay on the floor, he experienced a heavenly encounter with Jesus.

He went from being depressed, uninterested in God, and apathetic about church to being delivered and healed and having a face-to-face encounter with Jesus. All these experiences with God put such a supernatural fire in him that he was passionately testifying. This freedom, healing, and encounter were possible because his mom believed!

Sometimes a person is set free or healed without faith present, though this is less likely. Often, it is God's way of pursuing them. He has this grace where faith isn't always required because some haven't yet encountered His love. We love God after encountering His love. God wants us to meet Him and choose of our own free will whether to follow Him or not. He doesn't want us to just hear about Him and follow Him because others pressured us or our parents told us we should. In God's pursuit of His people, many times He reveals His love through His power.

This is how God pursued me, which led me to fall in love with Him and surrender everything. I was a believer my whole life, but it wasn't until age twenty-five that I encountered His power. Prior to that, I believed in God, and I believed He loved me, but it wasn't a "knowing," or a real understanding of the depth of His love. Much of my faith rested on "man's word for it" and my parents' faith.

> My message and my preaching were not with wise and persuasive words, but with a demonstration of the Spirit's power, so that your faith might not rest on human wisdom, but on God's power.
> —1 Corinthians 2:4–5

When I first encountered God in power, I truly met Jesus—and I fell in love! This love is what moved me to surrender my entire life to Him. I've never looked back.

Once I encountered God's power, my faith then rested on His power. His power is part of His nature. He is the King of the kingdom of God, and this kingdom is not a matter of talk but of power. It's like the difference between hearing about a person and their words through a mediator and then actually meeting the person in real life, where you can see their eyes, feel their handshake or hug, and hear their voice.

God reveals His love to people through His power in various ways. God may introduce Himself and reveal His love to some by setting them free. With almost every deliverance I witness week after week, the person's face has an expression of awe upon them being set free. You can just see that they've "looked into the eyes of Jesus." You can tell that they've encountered His love like never before.

At one service where I was ministering, a man who was said to need "emergency deliverance" was pushed onstage, but I could tell he didn't want to be there. He showed no desire to receive prayer and be set free. The Holy Spirit led me to say gently, "God wants to free you. But it's up to you. You have free will."

He hesitated for a while and then said, "I've been doing drugs for nineteen years. I've done a lot of bad things."

I began to pray for him, and as soon as I started declaring, a demon spoke out of him, "I'm not letting him go." I commanded the demons to leave him, and as soon as I did, the man started sobbing and holding his head in his hands. He was set free! He said, "I'm sorry, God," and continued to confess and repent. He apologized for crying and said, "I've never cried before. Men don't cry." I told him it's impossible not to cry in God's presence because His love is so big!

He confessed later that he came to the event intending

to stop the work of God. But God's grace is so big. In the same way that Jesus revealed His love to Saul as he was on his way to try to stop the move of God, God also revealed his love to this man.

A satanist used to come on every one of my live streams and speak the most vile and hateful things about Jesus and about me. The moderators blocked this woman from commenting, but she would relentlessly create new accounts and continue to write horrible things. One day God's power touched her through the screen as she was watching the live stream. She was delivered of depression and suicidal thoughts. (She had attempted suicide several times.) After receiving deliverance, she discovered God's love for her and gave her life to Him!

CAN YOU CAST DEMONS OUT OF SOMEONE WHO IS NOT SAVED?

As you can see in the above examples, you can absolutely cast demons out of nonbelievers! If you withhold deliverance from an unsaved person, you are also withholding God's love. When Jesus cast demons out of people, He never gave a prerequisite that they first confess the sinner's prayer. The Bible says that people came to Him, and He healed them. They came to Jesus out of curiosity, faith, or even skepticism, and He demonstrated His love by healing and delivering them.

Jesus says a mustard seed of faith can move mountains (Matt. 17:20). Do not belittle the mustard-seed size of faith in a person. For many, that's enough to remove the mountain of demonic oppression and spiritual blindness.

When a person comes into a church service where an anointed servant of God is ministering, they step into that vessel's spiritual territory. So many have testified of spiritual attacks that tried to keep them from coming to my church or a service where I was ministering. This is because the demons know that once the person steps into the church service (or turns on the live stream), they have stepped into my territory of spiritual authority where God's will must be done and the kingdom of heaven comes. That means demons must leave and people must be healed. Demons know their time is up when the individuals they're oppressing position themselves under the anointing.

To come to a church service or to watch a live stream where God's power is, is actually an act of faith itself. Remember, God counts actions, not feelings, as faith. You may even have thoughts and feelings of doubt, but you go to the church service anyway. That's faith!

The amount of faith that's needed for the miracle to happen is based on the person, case by case. A satanist who never had anyone tell them about Jesus may receive deliverance just by watching a live stream (with no faith and nothing but bad intentions). Delivering the person who never heard of Him may be how He introduces Himself to them and reveals His grace. On the other hand, God may require more faith to receive their miracles from a person who is already a believer.

> From everyone who has been given much, much will be demanded; and from the one who has been entrusted with much, much more will be asked.
> —LUKE 12:48

This statement means we cannot be lazy and disvalue God. Healing and deliverance are our inheritance as children of God. True children of God are surrendered and obedient to Him. When God instructs us to resist the devil's lies and believe, we need to do that with intentional action. We must live as true children of God to receive His benefits.

Keep in mind that one who is far from God yet receives deliverance may still need many more layers of deliverance. God may deliver a person from one layer of demonic oppression to reveal His love to them so they can follow Him, and then the rest of the deliverance and healing will come as that person walks in faith and obedience.

THE KEY OF SURRENDER

For complete deliverance and healing, surrender is key. If you have open doors to the devil, demons will just keep coming in. Keeping doors open to the devil also shows God that you don't value Him and His gifts, which blocks you from receiving miracles. You have the choice to be a sponge or a rock that sits in a stream. If you choose to be a sponge through surrender, you soak up all the anointing and will be completely healed and set free. But if you choose to be a rock (with doors open, living in sin), no matter how many times you're prayed for in the anointing, nothing will change. You'll never find the full inheritance without surrender. It's up to you to grab hold of your full inheritance of abundant life.

Chapter 7

WHAT MAKES DEMONS GO—
KEY 3: RENOUNCING

S I HAVE discussed, the main keys that unlock deliverance are (1) positioning yourself where the anointing is flowing and (2) having faith. When a high level of anointing is moving through a servant of God, in many cases that anointing and faith are the only keys needed. Yet what do I mean by "high level"?

DIFFERENT LEVELS OF ANOINTING

> We do not wrestle against flesh and blood, but against principalities, against powers, against the rulers of the darkness of this age, against spiritual hosts of wickedness in the heavenly places.
>
> —EPHESIANS 6:12, NKJV

This scripture is describing different levels of demonic powers, principalities being the highest level. The kingdom of darkness is a copying and twisting of the kingdom of God, using the same principles of the spiritual realm but for evil instead of good. The kingdom of God also has different levels of powers and authorities.

Fivefold ministers carry the highest levels of anointing, and apostles and prophets carry the very highest level as they are the foundation of the church, with Christ Jesus as the chief cornerstone (Eph. 2:20). There are two reasons for this arrangement. The fivefold ministers must carry the highest levels of anointing because (1) they are the ones who equip and pour into others and (2) they, especially the apostles and prophets, are required to minister in deliverance and deal with demonic powers, delivering the oppressed.

In the Book of Acts, the apostles were the main servants of God who were performing miracles by God's power:

> Everyone was filled with awe at the many wonders and signs performed by the apostles.
>
> —ACTS 2:43

> God did extraordinary miracles through Paul, so that even handkerchiefs and aprons that had touched him were taken to the sick, and their illnesses were cured and the evil spirits left them.
>
> —ACTS 19:11–12

God doing "extraordinary" miracles through Paul indicates that Paul carried extraordinary anointing—at a high level and more than usual.

The bigger the bonfire, the more you will feel the heat. The bigger the anointing, the more demons will feel the heat of that anointing. With a lesser level of anointing, demons may feel agitated and uncomfortable. They may start to manifest, but depending on whether the anointing level matches the demonic power level, the demons may or may not leave. Some people struggle to cast out demons, spending many hours and physical strength in the process. The main reason for this struggle is that either there is no anointing or not enough anointing to deal with the demonic power.

Mass deliverance—many people being delivered at once with little effort exercised by the servant of God—is an indication that a high-level anointing is operating through them. "You will know them by their fruits" (Matt. 7:16, NKJV). The fruits this verse speaks of are the fruits of character in the servant of God such as humility, love (including love for enemies), gentleness, self-control, and selflessness (Gal. 5:22–23). The word *fruits* also represents any healing, deliverance, salvation, and transformation taking place. When you see true testimonies, you know that the manifestations (falling back, screaming, coughing, crying, etc.) are true. You should judge not based only on manifestations but based on people's testimonies of true miracles and the changes happening in their lives.

It's very important that we operate not as individualistic, self-centered ministries but as the true kingdom that we are. We must identify where the present-day Peters and Pauls are, because some people can be set free only under a high-level anointing. These people are bound by principalities and/or complex oppression that only the high-level anointing can destroy.

In this revival we have entered, God has raised up modern-day Peters and Pauls. Open your eyes and see the great power of God that has been released on the earth. Do not get stuck in your bubble of traditional church. Do not close your eyes to the rest of the kingdom and a higher-level anointing that God needs you to position yourself under to be fully free and/or receive impartation.

The body of Christ needs to operate in unity as a true kingdom so that not a single believer remains stuck with demonic oppression. God has released the solution. His anointing is here. His anointed servants are releasing powerful anointing. Many pastors need to make sure their sheep are being fed properly by releasing them to receive the anointing they need, recognizing the gifts God has given the whole body of Christ: apostles and prophets, in addition to evangelists, pastors, and teachers.

THE KEY OF RENOUNCING

The next most prevalent key needed by many to unlock their deliverance is the key of renouncing. The definition of *renounce* is to "formally declare one's abandonment of (a claim, right, or possession)."[1] God has given you authority to accept either His will and portion for your life or the devil's will and portion. When you use your authority to accept only what God desires for your life, God's portion will manifest and you will see God's will being done in your life day by day. God's portion for you includes an inheritance of healing, freedom, and abundant life.

The devil's portion and desire for your life are the opposite of God's. The devil wants death, destruction, and lack. He wants you to live in bondage, sickness, and poverty. The way you walk in your authority to bring about God's will is to reject all the lies of the devil and the attacks that seem real, as if a life full of attacks and bondage is your portion. Before oppression and sickness can become the reality in your life, they begin in the spiritual realm as weapons formed against you that have not yet prospered.

No weapon formed against you shall prosper.
—ISAIAH 54:17, NKJV

Remember, we have free will. If we do not want weapons to prosper, we must do what God has called us to do and take authority over the weapons formed. We do not get to just live how we want, not doing anything in the spiritual realm while God stops all the weapons from prospering. We must decide whether we will allow the weapons to prosper. If we decide to take the action of walking in authority, then we will access God's power, and He will keep the weapons from prospering. But if we don't take that action and just allow the weapons to hit us, we disable God's help and enable the weapons to prosper.

> Submit yourselves, then, to God. Resist the devil, and he will flee from you.
>
> —JAMES 4:7

Resist the devil's lies and attacks coming as weapons in the spiritual realm, and then the weapons will not be able to prosper. Most oppression could've been stopped if one had resisted the devil's lies. For the most part this new-wine doctrine of understanding the power of your authority and how to walk in it has been missed in sermons and teaching across the body of Christ. Because of this lack of knowledge, many people have allowed demonic oppression to happen without knowing it.

For example, a spirit of anxiety doesn't immediately just enter a person; it is given access. It starts as a weapon—a lie from the enemy, speaking in the mind of the person, "Be afraid!" The way to have victory over this attack is to speak aloud, "I reject fear." You could also say, "I rebuke fear," or "I resist fear." The exact wording doesn't matter, just the meaning. You should then speak God's truth from

His Word. This is the action of accepting and claiming God's will and portion rather than the enemy's. Say out loud, "God has not given us a spirit of fear, but of power and of love and of a sound mind" (2 Tim. 1:7, NKJV). You could also say, "Jesus has promised me perfect peace in every circumstance. This is my inheritance from God, and it cannot be stolen from me." (See Isaiah 26:3.) By rejecting the devil's lies and declaring God's truth, you are carrying out the action of submitting to God.

If you take these actions when you are first attacked, the weapon cannot prosper. The devil must flee when we resist him and submit to God. It's a spiritual law.

In many cases sickness starts not in the physical realm but in the spiritual realm as a weapon. When you have symptoms of sickness, experience pain, or receive an unfavorable diagnosis from the doctor, immediately take the spiritual action to claim God's portion of healing. This action will give you victory over the devil's attempt to steal your health. Say out loud, "I reject all sickness," or "I reject this diagnosis," or "I reject this pain." This can be done after leaving the doctor's office; it doesn't have to be said immediately and in front of people. You can then declare, "By Jesus' stripes I am healed. Thank You, Jesus, for healing me." Once again, the exact words don't matter; the meaning is what's important.

Apply this principle of rejecting the devil's attacks and declaring God's truth to any kind of attack from the enemy—whether it has to do with addiction, your sleep, your mental health, your family, your finances, or the like.

> Those who belong to Christ Jesus have crucified
> the flesh with its passions and desires. Since we live
> by the Spirit, let us keep in step with the Spirit.
> —GALATIANS 5:24–25

Other important keys to having victory over demonic attacks involve denying your flesh, living by the Spirit, and keeping doors shut to the enemy (Eph. 4:27). If you've had an attack of anxiety, take inventory of what spiritual doors you may have opened that could have caused it. An anxiety attack doesn't always mean there's an open door, but often that is the case. Have you been watching horror movies, too much of the news, or perhaps too much commentary on politics? Have you been listening to the wrong voices that speak about their fear for the future? Have you been meditating on uncertainties and obstacles in your life? Make sure you deny your flesh's tendency to go by your feelings and thereby open doors to the enemy in these areas.

The temptation to intake more and more alcohol, sugar, coffee, social media, and other substances is a warning sign that the devil is trying to bind you with a spirit of addiction. If you sense these temptations, you must deny your flesh and fast whatever the temptation is. As for your health, make sure you're doing everything necessary to take good care of your body. If you're not getting enough sleep or eating poorly, you're opening the door for the devil to bring sickness. Keep your mouth always in alignment with God's truth. Never allow yourself to speak the thoughts and feelings that align with the devil's portion.

As I mentioned earlier, sometimes demonic oppression occurs because a family member in a previous generation, not the person themself, opened the door. Once authority is given to the enemy by opening doors and allowing the devil's portion, demonic oppression occurs. An important key to unlock this deliverance for many is to renounce—to do what should've been done before the oppression occurred, when it was in the stage of a "weapon formed against you."

To renounce is to reject the devil's portion in your life. It's like saying, "I used to accept the devil's portion by believing and declaring that I had _____ (anxiety, depression, a disease, insomnia, addiction, etc.). From now on, I no longer accept this as my portion. I reject _____. I now accept only God's portion for my life. I accept and receive my freedom and healing."

> Many of those who believed now came and openly confessed what they had done.
>
> —ACTS 19:18

This scripture reveals that the people choosing to follow Jesus were publicly renouncing. They were not confessing their sins openly just to be vulnerable and to "get them off their chests," so to speak. They were doing this to renounce, and this was a key in unlocking their deliverance.

RENOUNCING WEAKENS THE DEVIL'S GRIP

When you renounce, you are kicking the demon(s) out by saying, "I don't want you here, and you don't have a legal right to be here since I am a child of God. I am choosing God's will for my life." Remember, it's the anointing that destroys the yoke, so it's important to renounce any sin or open door when the anointing is present to deliver you. Otherwise, you could be renouncing and making the demons weaken to the point that they manifest but don't actually leave. In these situations demons could "play" with you, speaking through you and continually manifesting without leaving. This is why it's so crucial to be aligned with God's principles instead of casting out demons any old way.

There is not one example of a person delivering themself from a demon in the Bible. On the contrary Jesus told the disciples to cast out demons from others. Consider the fact that when a prisoner is in a jail cell, they cannot free themselves. They need someone with a key who is not in prison to unlock their deliverance.

When you know you need deliverance, take time with the Holy Spirit and allow Him to reveal all the things you need to renounce. In addition to renouncing the specific chains of oppression (addiction, sickness, anxiety, depression, etc.), it's important to renounce the open doors the oppression might have come through. If you've spoken words of death, agreeing with the devil's portion, *renounce speaking those words*. If you've claimed sickness as your portion, renounce doing that. If you watched videos or listened to music that brought anxiety or depression, renounce that. If you've been abused, renounce the abuse. If you've meditated on lies of the devil or sinful things, renounce that.

In whatever way you've sinned, renounce it. Set aside time to write a list of all that you need to renounce. Have the fear of God when making your renouncing list, taking it very seriously. For some, renouncing certain details is essential. That's why you should really take time with the Holy Spirit to allow Him to reveal all the things from your past that you need to renounce.

Five Types of Demonic Oppression

There are five different types of demonic oppression: demonic spirits (demons), generational curses, word curses, demonic soul ties, and demonic covenants. When a person is oppressed, they may have one, some, or all of these. The more complex the oppression, the more important it is to renounce. Everyone who is oppressed should renounce, whether or not it's technically needed for the deliverance to take place. Renouncing is simply walking in your authority and resisting the devil's grip in your life. It is also a part of repentance and making the decision to leave your sinful ways in the past so you can commit to following Jesus.

Renouncing Generational Curses

Some issues repeat generationally. For example, some families—no matter how hard they work from generation to generation—are stuck in poverty and can never get ahead. Some families see both father and son with addictions. Some see both mother and daughter having uncontrollable anxiety and panic attacks. Others find cancer repeating again and again in each generation. The reason for each of these scenarios is usually a generational curse.

You are connected to your past generations through your bloodline. If there was an open door in a previous generation, it may have permitted a generational curse to come on the whole family line. Remember, the enemy is allowed to have access only when he is given it. Generational curses happen because a door was opened in previous generations.

It's possible for a child to experience oppression. Some children have struggled with their identities since they were toddlers. Some children have had rage, demonic dreams, mental illness, or anxiety from a very young age. In many of these cases the root is a generational curse. If you recognize a struggle that is prevalent in many different family members over generations, most likely the root is a generational curse.

The way to be free of a generational curse is to renounce it, position yourself where true anointing is flowing, and believe! Jesus will destroy this generational curse for you and your family. Your children can be set free just by you seeking freedom from this generational curse. So often at my church services and events I've seen a parent start renouncing, and as soon as they do, their child or multiple children start manifesting! Sometimes demons scream out of the children. Other times they are coughing (being freed), and still other times the children fall back under the power of God.

After the parents finish renouncing, I declare the generational curse to be broken, and every time, Jesus immediately delivers the children as well as the parents! Many families have testified that after the curse was broken, the whole family experienced freedom and no longer had the oppression from the curse.

REAPING BLESSINGS VS. CURSES FOR YOUR LINEAGE

How joyful are those who fear the LORD and delight in obeying his commands. Their children will be successful everywhere; an entire generation of godly people will be blessed.

—PSALM 112:1–2, NLT

This scripture describes the principle of sowing and reaping. As you fear and serve God, you will reap blessings for your children. Because of free will, the opposite is also true. God has given humanity free will so that each person will decide whether to follow the Lord or the devil. If parents do not fear and serve God, they will not reap blessings for their children. The more the parents serve the enemy, the more they reap the enemy's portion for their children.

If you are a son or daughter of someone who served the enemy, there is nothing to fear or despair. When you come to Jesus, He destroys the works of the devil in your life and frees you from generational curses or whatever demonic reaping has come on your life due to your parents or past generational sins. The point many believers miss is that you must follow God's ways to receive total deliverance. In most cases, generational curses don't automatically break as soon as you confess that Jesus is Lord. You need to position yourself where the anointing is flowing for the anointing to destroy the yoke. If you know the details of the open doors of your parents and past generations, include them in your renouncing list.

RENOUNCING WORD CURSES

A word curse is an oppression that comes from words spoken by yourself or another person.

> The tongue can bring death or life; those who love
> to talk will reap the consequences.
> —PROVERBS 18:21, NLT

The second part of this verse means that those who talk carelessly, speaking whatever they feel, will reap bad consequences. The devil brings thoughts and emotions sometimes, and when you speak those negative thoughts and emotions, you can be cursing yourself. The more you speak a negative word, the more you are allowing the devil access to bring a curse through that word. You have the power to bring "death" to your life by speaking negative words.

If you speak the opposite of what your identity in Christ is, the wrong feelings and in some cases sexual attractions will become stronger and can turn into oppression. If you speak that you'll never get a job and will always be poor, you're opening the door for demonic oppression to come in that area, supernaturally blocking you from getting a job and making money. If you speak that you'll get the same sickness that family members have, you're opening the door for that sickness to come. If you say you don't have what it takes to do what God is calling you to do, you may find there is a supernatural force that is always trying to pull you away from God's will.

Renounce whatever words of death you remember speaking in the past. Whatever you remember speaking that goes against God's Word and truth you should renounce to ensure any word curse is broken off.

It's also important to renounce negative words that have been spoken to you. Many people have so many negative words attached to them in the spiritual realm because they've never rejected the words of death that people spoke to them. Sometimes the weapons formed against you come in the form of words spoken by others. You need to take action and reject those words so those weapons do not prosper.

Take time with the Holy Spirit and make a list of all the negative words you can remember that were spoken to you, about you, and about your future. I encourage you to pause and take time to write this list. In chapter 10 I will declare all these words and curses to leave your life in Jesus' name. Take as long as you need to make this list before continuing to read.

WHAT ARE SOUL TIES?

Another kind of oppression is demonic soul ties. Soul ties form within any close relationship. A literal spiritual connection happens between any two people who are close. There are good, godly soul ties, and there are bad soul ties. Examples of godly soul ties include these:

1. Between a husband and wife

> He said, "'This explains why a man leaves his father and mother and is joined to his wife, and the two are united into one.' Since they are no longer two but one, let no one split apart what God has joined together."
>
> —MATTHEW 19:5–6, NLT

2. Between a spiritual parent and a spiritual son or daughter

> For this reason I have sent Timothy to you, who is my beloved and faithful son in the Lord, who will remind you of my ways in Christ, as I teach everywhere in every church.
>
> —1 CORINTHIANS 4:17, NKJV

In the way Paul wrote about Timothy, you can see a closeness in the spiritual realm for the purpose of the kingdom. The love Paul showed Timothy in pouring into him was also a love for God's people, as Paul knew that many more of God's people would be built up and ministered to as he imparted the anointing in Timothy and equipped Timothy to be a powerful vessel of God.

3. In God-ordained friendships

> When David had finished speaking to Saul, the soul of Jonathan was bonded to the soul of David, and Jonathan loved him as himself.
>
> —1 SAMUEL 18:1, AMP

The actual soul of Jonathan was bonded to David. And Jonathan's love for David was supernatural, especially because this was a pure relationship. Usually we hear of one person loving another as themself only when it's husband and wife. But this relationship was supernatural—the soul tie was pure, godly, powerful, and for the purpose of God's kingdom.

Jonathan didn't love David because David had a great personality and was fun to be around. Jonathan loved David because God led him to. God led Jonathan to recognize the important work He was doing through David and to see David with His eyes. Imagine how God sees His servants who through surrender and obedience allow Him to do all He wants through them, showing love to His people and freeing and healing them. This is a special and passionate love that God has for His servants.

So, Jonathan was seeing David with God's eyes, and that is how he could love David so supernaturally. God knew that David needed a godly man who would serve him and help him fulfill his God-given assignment. Therefore, God placed these two together to accomplish His plans. This soul tie was so strong that it prevented the devil from tearing David and Jonathan apart. There was a supernatural force that kept them together for God's purposes.

Renouncing Demonic Soul Ties

> Do not be deceived: "Bad company corrupts good morals."
> —1 Corinthians 15:33, AMP

If you form a close relationship with the wrong person, your good morals will be corrupted. One who believes they have willpower and is serious about their good moral standards may say, "I can be strong enough to not let that person corrupt me." But this scripture is speaking of a supernatural principle in the spiritual realm that takes place when you allow the wrong person in close. A demonic soul tie will be formed. When that happens, you are literally connected to this person, and their corruption in your life will be inevitable.

> Do not be unequally bound together with unbelievers [do not make mismatched alliances with them, inconsistent with your faith]. For what partnership can righteousness have with lawlessness? Or what fellowship can light have with darkness? What harmony can there be between Christ and Belial (Satan)? Or what does a believer have in common with an unbeliever? What agreement is there between the temple of God and idols? For we are the temple of the living God; just as God said: "I will dwell among them and walk among them; and I will be their God, and they shall be My people. So come out from among unbelievers

and be separate," says the Lord, "And do not touch what is unclean; and I will graciously receive you and welcome you [with favor]."

—2 Corinthians 6:14–17, amp

This scripture speaks of the seriousness of being unequally yoked in any kind of relationship. To be in an unequally yoked relationship is to have a big open door to the enemy and can lead to a demonic soul tie forming.

The one unequally yoked relationship that God allows in special circumstances is marriage. If one becomes saved after marriage and the husband or wife is not, or if both begin marriage as lukewarm Christians and only one becomes surrendered, God's grace is available for these relationships. The Christian spouse can pray and believe for salvation for the other spouse.

Each circumstance is different and should be dealt with case by case, led by the Holy Spirit. For example, when a husband or wife of their own free will keeps denying Jesus over a long period of time, the believing spouse needs wisdom from the Holy Spirit to know which direction to go regarding the marriage.

If you are in a marriage where your spouse is not saved or is lukewarm, know that God's grace is covering you, yet at the same time, be vigilant in the spirit. If you are not serious about continual obedience to God and steadfast to reject the devil's lies, it will be easy for the enemy to bring oppression to you from the unbelieving spouse's influence. You must be serious about consistently rejecting the devil's lies and remaining focused on Jesus, filling yourself with His Word.

Do You Have a Demonic Soul Tie?

The major sign that you have a demonic soul tie with someone is when you sense manipulation through them. This person might want to control you, so they manipulate you to do as they please, threatening emotional or physical abuse. If you feel pressure to please a certain person but you don't have that people-pleasing feeling toward others, it's a sign that you have a demonic soul tie.

Perhaps you are serious about always pleasing God in every circumstance except when it comes to situations with this person. Perhaps you have given in to temptation or could see yourself doing so to please this person. You may feel anxiety at the thought of this person being disappointed with you. In romantic relationships, often demonic soul ties are the reason why some keep going back to abusive boyfriends or girlfriends or to partners they know aren't good for them.

Demonic soul ties can form in romantic relationships, friendships, and mentorships. Once you recognize a demonic soul tie in your life, it is very important to renounce it. Speak aloud declarations such as "I don't want to be controlled by this person. I don't want to care what this person thinks. I don't want to be in a relationship with this person anymore. I renounce this soul tie."

Sometimes physical objects can carry a demonic force, helping to keep a demonic soul tie intact. Jewelry given by the one you are connected to can carry demonic attachments. At times when I minister, a person will renounce a demonic soul tie and then take off their ring, and immediately the power of God touches them, and they are set free. It's important that you allow the Holy Spirit to reveal any objects a person gave you that may have demonic attachments. You should renounce these and throw them away, while positioning yourself where anointing is flowing. Anointing is flowing out of this book. In chapter 10 I will pray for you, and God will set you free from demonic soul ties, if that is the freedom you need.

PHYSICAL OBJECTS WITH DEMONIC ATTACHMENTS

> A number who had practiced sorcery brought their scrolls together and burned them publicly. When they calculated the value of the scrolls, the total came to fifty thousand drachmas. In this way the word of the Lord spread widely and grew in power.
>
> —ACTS 19:19–20

As noted above, some objects may have demonic attachments. All witchcraft items such as tarot cards carry demonic attachments, as do objects used for New Age practices. Some jewelry with symbols such as the evil eye have demonic roots, pointing to other gods, and may carry demonic attachments. Objects of idols are also examples.

Again, items given with the intention to manipulate may carry demonic attachments too. There may be times when a person tries to give you a gift and something feels off about it. Perhaps the person is pushy and trying to force a relationship with you. Maybe you've seen red flags in a person such as jealousy, so it seems strange that they're giving you a gift or some food. In these types of situations it's best not to eat the food or accept the gift. (In most cases it's fine to take the gift in the gift giver's presence but shortly afterward renounce it and throw it away.)

Demonic attachments can come on a variety of objects. Take some time with the Holy Spirit, allowing Him to show you which objects should be discarded and the best way to throw them out or even burn them. You can gather these items and prepare a trash bag to throw them away as I pray for you in chapter 10.

Renouncing Demonic Covenants

Covenants are very powerful in the spiritual realm, whether they are godly or demonic. Examples of godly covenants include promises or commitments to serve God your whole life, to be planted where God has called you, and to be a spiritual son or daughter to your spiritual parent (such as how Elisha made a covenant with Elijah), as well as covenants of marriage. When you make a godly covenant through words, a powerful supernatural force from God protects it and makes it concrete.

There are also demonic covenants. Practicing witchcraft is the action of signing up to be a servant of the devil. Higher degrees of covenants occur in witchcraft as well, depending on what level of service to the devil a person commits to. Then there are covenants of death that people make, many times unknowingly. When a person says, "I want to die," or something similar, that is an action in the spiritual realm of making a covenant with the devil, giving him authority to send a demon to influence that person to kill themselves.

If you've ever made a demonic covenant, it's crucial that you renounce it by saying, "I renounce making the covenant that I would _____." If you've ever said that you wanted to die and/or made suicidal attempts, you should say something like "I renounce saying I wanted to die. I renounce meditating on killing myself. I renounce making plans and attempting to kill myself. I want to live. I choose to follow Jesus."

As I mentioned earlier, when true anointing is present, most demons leave quickly and easily. It's not necessary that every single person must renounce, because the anointing is so powerful that many demons cannot even fight. There are lower-level demons, higher-level demons, and levels in between. In some cases, multiple demons are in a person, and in others, just one. At times, there is complex bondage, such as when a person has given a lot of authority to the devil. A person who has served the devil by practicing witchcraft usually has a more complex bondage than a person who has not.

Sometimes a demon will leave as I'm preaching. I've heard several individuals testify that they felt demons leave them during the sermon as they sat in their seats, and they were free! Additionally, often in the middle of my sermon a demon will start to speak, yell, or manifest in some other way in a person. This also happened as Jesus ministered:

> Then Jesus went to Capernaum, a town in Galilee, and taught there in the synagogue every Sabbath day. There, too, the people were amazed at his teaching, for he spoke with authority.
>
> Once when he was in the synagogue, a man possessed by a demon—an evil spirit—cried out, shouting, "Go away! Why are you interfering with us, Jesus of Nazareth? Have you come to destroy us? I know who you are—the Holy One of God!"
>
> But Jesus reprimanded him. "Be quiet! Come out of the man," he ordered. At that, the demon threw

the man to the floor as the crowd watched; then it came out of him without hurting him further.

Amazed, the people exclaimed, "What authority and power this man's words possess! Even evil spirits obey him, and they flee at his command!"

—LUKE 4:31–36, NLT

When a demon speaks or yells out of a person as I'm preaching, I follow Jesus' example. I pause the sermon for a moment and confront the demon, commanding it to go. And glory to God, the demons always go! I then continue preaching.

These types of demons that can't even make it through the sermon are lower-level demons. They don't have as strong a grip as other demons. It is amazing to realize that just by attending a church service where God is moving in power through a vessel, you could be set free before someone prays for you. Or you can watch a service online and be free as soon as you tune in, even without someone praying over you. This is the incredible power of God that's available right now to anyone who will just come like a child and receive.

When I begin to declare that demons must go, whether praying for people individually or corporately, many demons leave immediately. These demons make it through the sermon, but once authority is executed with words, they lose their grip and are evicted. Other demons seem more stubborn, responding with a no when I command them to go. In some of these cases, the demons aren't very powerful; they are just trying with all their might to make one last shot before they know their time is up. It's like when a child whines when a parent asks them to do a chore. The whining doesn't allow the child to get out of what they have to do; it just prolongs the process a bit.

But other demons that come with resistance actually are higher-level demons, or the oppression is complex; therefore, more keys need to be used to unlock the deliverance. This may involve renouncing a demonic covenant. When a demon speaks out of a person "I own her/him," it usually means the person has made a demonic covenant. Demons say such words because the person has given them the legal right to bring death to the person's life. In the past, the person made the decision to give the demon authority. The person needs to relinquish that authority by renouncing so the demons lose their legal right to stay.

I must mention, however, that you should not rely on demons to give you spiritual insight because demons can lie. Jesus sometimes asked demons a question and they responded with the truth because Jesus was always led by the Holy Spirit and properly walking in His authority. Demons lie when one diverts from walking in their authority and begins to give them too much attention.

In situations where renouncing is a necessary key for a person's deliverance, it is as if the demons' grip over them is loosened when they renounce. And then as the anointed servant of God commands the demons to go, the anointing is like a blast of fire that forces them out. Renouncing is like unlocking the chains around you, and then the anointing lifts the heavy unlocked chains off you.

With this new insight of the oppression you may have, you will now be able to renounce in detail to unlock your deliverance. Take time with the Holy Spirit to develop your renouncing list. As you seek your deliverance, remember that it's not always a onetime deliverance that brings complete freedom. For some, the Holy Spirit will deliver layer by layer as He reveals more and more items that you need to renounce and as you move closer to full surrender (if you aren't already at that place).

We will discuss one more important type of bondage, as well as the open doors that lead to this bondage, in depth in the following chapter.

Chapter 8

THE REALITY OF WITCHCRAFT

THERE ARE TWO kinds of spirituality: spiritual life led by God or spiritual life led by the devil. When it comes to the supernatural, there are only two sources: God's power or the devil's power. A neutral spiritual life or a neutral supernatural power does not exist. Every human is made in God's image and likeness. Because of this, young children do not automatically desire evil. All humans have a natural tendency toward goodness. It's when they start being persuaded by the devil through the wrong people, media, or other influences that some desire less and less goodness.

For example, when a tragedy such as a plane crash or a mass shooting occurs, most people around the world don't delight in it but instead grieve over it. Showing genuine empathy and desiring good for all people are their natural inclinations. The devil knows that most people don't desire evil, so he has sneakily enticed people into the darkness of "spiritual practices" without them knowing they are partnering with darkness.

> And no wonder, for Satan himself masquerades as an angel of light.
>
> —2 CORINTHIANS 11:14

This scripture means that the devil leads people to evil in a "moral-looking" package. The devil disguises himself as an angel of light in many ways. One huge way is through other religions and other spiritual practices. The Father, the Son (Jesus), and the Holy Spirit—the three in one—are God; there is no other true God. The spirit behind the god of Buddha is a demonic spirit, not a holy spirit. The same is true for the gods of all other religions. When people worship a god that is not Jesus, they automatically open the door to the devil and allow him to have authority over their lives and to bring demonic oppression.

If you have ever worshipped another god, it's vital that you renounce doing so and renounce all the rituals and practices you participated in with that religion. If you had idols or objects that represented these gods (such as a Buddha statue), renounce these items and anything you did with them. Then dispose of them by either throwing them away or burning them.

Worshipping other gods is an open door for generational curses. Sometimes an important key that breaks the generational curse on a family is renouncing the worship of other gods in the family line—renouncing on behalf of your family members in previous generations.

New Age Practices

All non-Christian spiritual practices that invoke supernatural powers are an open door to the devil. When you seek God, you receive His Holy Spirit to help you. When a person seeks such things as healing, energy, insight for the future, and a "higher consciousness," they are receiving demons to give them these powers. Demonic powers are the devil's counterfeit to the anointing.

Psychics: counterfeit to prophets

A prophet gets insight into the future from God's power (the anointing working inside the prophet). A psychic gets their insight from demons.

When you're a believer who is surrendered and abiding by God's ways, including being planted at a church that provides a covering of protection (anointing flowing from the leader to the rest of the church), demons cannot follow you places and observe you. However, if you speak somewhere publicly where demons are in other people, they can hear what you say.

If a person is not a surrendered believer, demons may be oppressing that person and therefore can report to other demons, as they're part of one kingdom. Just as believers speak to other believers and angels operate together with God and not on their own accord, demons work together as a part of their united demonic kingdom. When a person is oppressed, the demon can hear the words they speak. Also, if a person is not oppressed by a demon but is speaking words of death (negative confessions), it is as if they are speaking on the devil's "radio frequency." When a person speaks negatively, the devil can often hear.

Psychics use their knowledge from demons to speak things that they could not know without a supernatural power. To build trust, the psychics speak something into a person's future to entice them to keep coming. They are partnering with the enemy to declare what the enemy wants for the person's future. If a person does not repent, renounce, and take authority over what the psychic spoke, that "prediction" can truly happen.

Sometimes the psychic will speak "good" things about one's future. That's all an allure of the devil, disguising himself as an angel of light so the person will keep listening to the psychic and paying them (which is sowing into the devil's kingdom).

Tarot cards also utilize demonic powers for spiritual insight and direction. When a person uses tarot cards, they are opening the door to demons. Looking to horoscopes for spiritual insight falls in this category as well. The different horoscopes represent gods and goddesses that are found in Hindu, Egyptian, and Greek cultures. The source behind every false god (anything other than Jesus) is a demon. If you are looking to horoscopes for direction and insight, you are actually looking to demons.

When you intentionally seek out horoscopes to give you direction and insight, it opens a door to a demon. If you're watching a news talk show and someone mentions what their horoscope of the day is, that does not open the door. It is the action of seeking out your horoscope for insight and direction in your life that allows a demon access. If in the past you casually read a horoscope in a magazine but did not take it to heart, that does not open a door to a demon. However, it's always best to err on the side of caution and renounce if you're unsure whether you have opened a door.

Reiki and crystals: counterfeit to the laying on of hands and to healing by God's power

Reiki is a Japanese "healing technique" that claims to manipulate the body's energy flow and promote relaxation. The word *Reiki* is made up of the Japanese words *rei*, which means "universal," and *ki*, which means "vital life force energy."[1] This supernatural energy force is a demonic power. If a person performs or receives a Reiki healing, they have invited the demonic power to bring "healing."

Using crystals with the belief that they will bring

healing is also inviting demonic powers. God made crystals, but He didn't make them to be used as a medium to heal. Jesus is the only healer. We are to seek only God's power for healing, no other object or force.

At times, God may lead an anointed vessel to release the anointing on something like a handkerchief, as Paul did (Acts 19:11), but that is a true anointed vessel doing so. In a situation like this, the anointed vessel is releasing God's power on the object—so that it is not the object itself but Jesus' power that a person seeks for healing. Those who seek crystals for healing are seeking the objects, not the person of Jesus. When you seek a supernatural power that is not Jesus, it automatically opens a door to demons.

New Age meditation and manifesting: counterfeits to biblical principles

> Keep this Book of the Law always on your lips; meditate on it day and night, so that you may be careful to do everything written in it. Then you will be prosperous and successful.
>
> —JOSHUA 1:8

Meditating on God's Word is an important way to stay focused and strong spiritually. Meditating on God's Word and whatever is good (Phil. 4:8) makes you more spiritual in the sense that it makes you more like Jesus. It opens your ears and eyes to hear and see God more clearly. Those who meditate in the New Age way (without believing in Jesus) are meditating to become more "spiritual" and have their "spiritual understanding unlocked." They open themselves up and invite "energy" to fill them.

UNLOCK YOUR DELIVERANCE

When people seek an "energy" or supernatural force that is not Jesus, they open themselves up to demonic forces.

The New Age practice called manifesting—the idea of using positive thoughts as energy to attract or create positive experiences[2]—is also demonic. Manifesting is another biblical principle that the devil has twisted. Knowing the power of God's principles, the devil twists them and makes counterfeits so that people are deceived by the "results." When people use biblical principles outside of faith in Jesus, they'll find that the principles "work" because they are spiritual laws, like $1 + 2 = 3$. But when they do this outside Jesus' ways, they open doors to demons, and the "blessings" they receive come with sorrow. The blessings are not protected. Therefore, all the things they receive from New Age manifesting come from a demonic root and could be foiled at any time.

Those who choose to keep believing in their dreams, speaking positively, and working toward their goals will probably see positive results. They will most likely achieve their dreams because they are applying biblical principles. However, if the blessing of receiving the dream did not come with God's help, it does not carry His protection. The dream achieved through manifesting could either crumble or remain intact, but the person can't even enjoy the fulfillment of it because they are tormented by demons. In contrast, God's blessings come without sorrow (Prov. 10:22).

Yoga: counterfeit to being yoked to Jesus

Yoga is another New Age practice that can open doors to demons. *Yoga* comes from a Sanskrit word meaning "yoke" or "union" and describes "a group of physical,

106

mental, and spiritual practices or disciplines that originated in ancient India" and aim to control (yoke) and still the mind.[3]

Yoga originated in Hinduism. Its origin is not merely cultural but religious—worshipping a false god (demon). Since *yoga* means "yoke," we have to ask, "Yoke to what?" It's a yoking or "uniting the mind and body with universal energy."[4] Remember that any "energy" or supernatural force that is not the power of God (Jesus) is demonic. So yoga literally means yoking oneself to demonic forces. The poses, which are named after Hindu gods, were originally created to worship these gods and invite their "energy" into one's body to give peace, energy, and spiritual insight. Kundalini yoga specifically invokes the kundalini spirit; those who engage in that activity invite and desire this spirit to come into their bodies and make movements.[5]

If you as a Christian attend a yoga class without the intention to worship other gods or invite demonic forces in, is it OK? Many think so, but honestly, it is dangerous spiritually, like playing with fire. It is like leaving the door unlocked. There is no guarantee that a robber will enter, but why take the risk? The origin and source behind the practice are demonic. So it's best not to practice yoga at all and not do yoga poses. There are other ways to stretch and many other positions you can move your body in for exercise and wellness.

Seeking protection outside of Jesus invites demons

Every practice so far mentioned is a portal that accesses demons. Coming to the altar at church and seeking Jesus anytime in your life is a portal (door) to God's kingdom, where you access the Holy Spirit and miracles from Jesus. When you participate in counterfeit altars, you access the demonic spiritual world, and that is where demons can come and gain access in a person's life.

Another portal that opens the door to demons is burning sage for "protection." When people burn sage, they do it to "keep evil energy away." Yet they are actually doing the opposite—inviting demons in. There are other practices that people believe are bringing protection when they are actually invoking demons, including wearing evil-eye jewelry. Another practice is hanging dream catchers with the belief that they will stop bad dreams and protect the person from evil.

If you have ever done any of these New Age practices, renounce them, and Jesus will deliver you!

PRACTICING WITCHCRAFT

The devil invites and persuades people to serve him, and practicing witches and warlocks are realities. He entices them with success, fame, money, and sometimes "love" from him (which he can never give). Some people surrender themselves to the devil in exchange for their desires to be fulfilled. The devil has supernatural powers to give them success, fame, and money, but his "blessings" will always come with sorrow. These so-called gifts come with the cost of torment from demons and eternity in hell—that is, if a person does not repent and give their life to Jesus.

You may notice that some people are miserable even though they have success and money. The reason so many celebrities and other wealthy people commit suicide is that their "blessings" came with the sorrow of tormenting demons of depression and death.

When people serve the devil, they bring death and destruction. Some make human sacrifices. Witches and warlocks send demons to people and send curses. A person doesn't "catch" a demon by being in a place where demons are cast out. That's a lie from the devil to try to keep people from coming to where the power of God is flowing and from seeking deliverance, for fear of "catching" other demons. Demons actually come from the act of witches and warlocks sending them when there is legal authority (open doors)—that is the devil's system.

Witches and warlocks have the authority to send demons and curses only when someone opens a door in the spiritual realm. Once a person chooses to give the devil a foothold and thus grants them permission, a witch or warlock sends a demon. An open door can also occur when a person visits a witch or warlock and pays them to either curse or put a "love spell" on another. If the intended recipient is not a believer or is a believer with open doors, the witch or warlock has authority to send those spells and curses on that person.

There are also witch doctors, so-called "healers" who use magic. The magic is actually demonic power. Usually after a person goes to a witch doctor, they find their issue goes away, but then another issue appears that is much more severe. At other times the issue goes away for a while but then comes back with worse problems. In these cases demons have come to oppress the person, and that is why their issue is worse than before they went to the witch doctor or "healer."

If you have ever gone to a witch, warlock, or witch doctor, it is very important to renounce that encounter and the specific actions you took as advised by the practitioner. I've seen many people set free upon renouncing visits to demonic "healers," as well as children immediately set free once their parents renounced taking them to such practitioners.

If you've ever practiced witchcraft, it's crucial you renounce in-depth. Renounce all the curses, spells, and demonic acts you did to others. Renounce the demonic covenant you made with the devil. Throw away all the witchcraft objects and materials you have. If you've practiced witchcraft, it's critical that you take surrendering to Jesus seriously. And you must be patient in your deliverance journey. When a person has practiced witchcraft, there usually is more than one layer of demonic oppression, and many times God delivers layer by layer. The enemy is not happy when one who was on his side turns to Jesus. Be aware of this so you never let your guard down and never give the devil an inch. Take the actions of maintaining your deliverance very seriously. I'll discuss how to maintain your deliverance in the chapters ahead.

Chapter 9

WHAT MAKES DEMONS
GO—KEY 4: SOWING

OWING INTO GOD's kingdom is a command from God and a principle that releases different kinds of blessings and heavenly resources. It is extremely powerful. The devil has blinded many believers from seeing the true power in a seed that is sown into God's kingdom. Sowing can even have a connection to deliverance at times. In this chapter I will release revelation from the Holy Spirit that will open your eyes to see the power that lies in your seed and what sowing unlocks.

THE PRINCIPLE OF SOWING

Giving to a church, particularly God's true church where He has anointed and commissioned a servant of God to establish and lead the congregation, has great spiritual significance. Many people think of giving to a church as just donating to help with its costs, especially since churches are nonprofits and donations are the only way for them to pay their expenses. Yet giving accomplishes much more than just donating. Many are unaware of the depths of power that come through giving.

Giving is especially powerful when you sow into a church that is truly anointed by God, and this should be an important reason you give generously. It is your responsibility as a believer to contribute to the work of God. Your offering also acts as a thanksgiving to the ministry you have freely received from.

Women and other disciples contributed financially out of their own means to Jesus' ministry (Luke 8:1–3). Because they gave, the work of God could move forward and more people could be reached. Today it is the same. Your seed means that more of the work of God can go forth. Your seed translates to many more souls being saved, healed, delivered, and touched by God through the ministry. Catch the revelation of what a powerful act you're doing for God's kingdom every time you sow! Your giving also makes God proud.

At the same time, the power of your seed has even more dimensions that are critical for you to understand. The more revelation you have of the power of your seed, the more you will always be willing to give the amount God desires you to give. As the title of this chapter conveys, the best way to think of giving is as *sowing*.

> Do not be deceived, God is not mocked; for whatever a man sows, that he will also reap.
> —GALATIANS 6:7, NKJV

Sowing can take many different forms. For example, you can sow kindness or cruelty with your actions or words. If you sow kindness, you will reap kindness from other people; they will be kind back to you because you are kind first and their hearts are moved to reciprocate that. The same is true for sowing cruelty: if you sow cruelty, you will reap cruelty. But also, in the spiritual realm, when you sow kindness, you will generally reap God's favor. You may even experience supernatural favor from people before you have a chance to be kind to them. You can also sow your time and gifts as you serve God, and you will reap spiritual blessings because of those seeds.

One major way of sowing that God commands so we can reap is giving financially to God's kingdom through His church. This is not the only way to sow, but it should not be neglected or substituted. If so, you will miss out on the reaping God intended to release to you through your sowing.

> "Bring all the tithes (the tenth) into the storehouse, so that there may be food in My house, and test Me now in this," says the LORD of hosts, "if I will not open for you the windows of heaven and pour out for you [so great] a blessing until there is no more room to receive it."
>
> —MALACHI 3:10, AMP

This scripture details the principle of sowing and reaping. God is saying in this verse that He has so many blessings you won't have room for them all. God also reveals how these blessings transpire. They do not come by praying, fasting, or doing good works. These specific blessings come when you bring your offering to the church, also called sowing. God desires to give you so many blessings, miracles, and supernatural resources, and He will pour them out to you as you obey Him.

Some miracles come as you obey Him by making the sacrifice of time, lifting your faith, and going to church (or attending online). Your actions of sacrificing and coming with faith release miracles to you. Other blessings and miracles come as you obey God in your day-to-day life. He rewards you for obeying Him, seeking Him, and living by His Spirit. Still other blessings come as you serve Him in His work.

Many have testified that as they served God at 5F Church, they noticed oppression breaking off their lives, experienced sudden breakthroughs, and could do things they've never done before. Others testified that as they served God, the desires of the world fell away and they were transformed more into Christ's image. Still others testified that God released blessings and miracles through their financial sowing. In each scenario God released blessings in response to a person's obedience, surrender, and sacrifice.

When you seek Him, you will find Him. As you seek Him and follow His ways, you will discover the abundant rewards of being a child of God and the inheritance that is yours.

Salvation is free, but a life of miracles, blessings, and abundance does not come to a believer who is luke-warm (meaning neither hot nor cold about their faith; see Revelation 3:15–16). They might receive some bless-ings and miracles, but not a daily life of abundance and miracles. You access the reward of being a child of God through obedience. God's miracles have value. They are not cheap.

> He is a rewarder of those who diligently seek Him.
> —HEBREWS 11:6, NKJV

Stop and read that verse again. He is a rewarder of *those who diligently seek Him.* So, His rewards are not free. The cost is obedience to His Word, which includes giving financially to His church.

Do you not know that those who officiate in the
sacred services of the temple eat from the temple
[offerings of meat and bread] and those who regularly attend the altar have their share from the
[offerings brought to the] altar? So also [on the
same principle] the Lord directed those who preach
the gospel to get their living from the gospel.
—1 CORINTHIANS 9:13–14, AMP

Soon afterward Jesus began a tour of the nearby
towns and villages, preaching and announcing the
Good News about the Kingdom of God. He took
his twelve disciples with him, along with some
women who had been cured of evil spirits and diseases. Among them were Mary Magdalene, from
whom he had cast out seven demons; Joanna, the
wife of Chuza, Herod's business manager; Susanna;
and many others who were contributing from their
own resources to support Jesus and his disciples.
—LUKE 8:1–3, NLT

In the above scriptures, God led these people to contribute financially to Jesus' ministry, which was able to
advance because of the offerings given. God commands us
to give to the church so that the ministry can go forth with
excellence. If you are disobedient in that, you are being
disobedient to God. You are missing out on a reaping that
comes through sowing into the kingdom of God. If you
are unable to earn money because of your youth, a dis-
ability, or another reason, there are exceptions for you.
However, if you choose to be in a season of unemploy-
ment out of laziness, that grace does not extend to you.

> Make it your goal to live a quiet life, minding your own business and working with your hands, just as we instructed you before. Then people who are not believers will respect the way you live, and you will not need to depend on others.
>
> —1 Thessalonians 4:11–12, nlt

> But if anyone does not provide for his relatives, and especially for members of his household, he has denied the faith and is worse than an unbeliever.
>
> —1 Timothy 5:8, esv

> For even when we were with you, we would give you this command: If anyone is not willing to work, let him not eat.
>
> —2 Thessalonians 3:10, esv

God instructs us to give to the work of His kingdom for at least two reasons. First, the finances we give enable the work of God to go forth with excellence. Not contributing generously to the kingdom of God (when you have the ability to) is equal to not caring about the work of God. It is equal to not caring about souls being saved; hearing the gospel; and being healed, delivered, and equipped to have victory over the devil. The church is where the majority of this work takes place. Those who are sent into the world to be a light to the lost are discipled in the church and receive impartation there. The church is the foundation and source of the necessary work of God for the whole body of Christ.

Second, giving our money to God is a part of surrendering our entire lives. God wants you to rid yourself of selfishness and all idols. If you find it difficult to give money to God's work because you'd rather spend it on yourself, money has become an idol in your life.

In Matthew 19:21, Jesus tells the rich man whose idol was money that he must give all his riches away to obtain salvation. This is not an instruction for every wealthy person. It was Jesus' instruction to this particular man because money had an idolatrous hold on him. If you are not generous in giving to God's work, money has a hold on you. God wants you to get to the place where if you had hundreds of thousands of dollars and He asked you to give it all away, you would be OK with that. This would reveal that money does not have any grip on you.

The truth is that all your money should belong to God, not just 10 percent (the tithe). You are able to have a job only because of God. Any way you have acquired money has been possible only through God. Yes, you played a part by working hard, but your hard work is very small in comparison to the part God played. He created the whole universe, including the existence of jobs for productive employment. He created you and gave you the ability to show up and do the work. Then He opened doors and gave you favor to get the job.

When you reflect on these truths, you can see how silly it is to think you deserve all your earned money (besides the 10 percent that goes to the church). God wants you to begin to see that all your money belongs to Him—that you're just a steward of what He's entrusted you with for His kingdom purposes. The only way your heart can be transformed to this level of selflessness is for you to give sacrificially and generously.

For your heart will always pursue what you esteem
as your treasure.
—MATTHEW 6:21, TPT

This verse shows that if you choose to put your treasure in the kingdom of God, your heart will follow. If you consider material possessions rather than God's kingdom to be your treasure, your heart will also follow in that direction. You must show you value the work of God by contributing financially to it. When you give generously to the work of God, your heart and your treasure will both align with God and His kingdom.

Many people grumble when ministers speak about giving. Yet these church leaders have a responsibility to instruct you to do what the Word says. God isn't worried about the church receiving enough finances, though that is important. He's more concerned with your heart. He's more concerned about you sacrificing and surrendering all—even your finances—so your heart can be transformed and belong completely to Him.

THE SOWING-DELIVERANCE CONNECTION

Giving to God's work is also important because at times there is a connection between sowing and deliverance. As we noted earlier, sowing into God's kingdom brings a reaping. Sometimes it's appropriate to give to God just out of thanksgiving. Sometimes you will feel moved to give just out of obedience. But at the same time, it's important to remember the principle of sowing and reaping. Whenever you sow into God's kingdom, you *will* reap.

The reaping comes in the form of spiritual and physical blessings, such as provision. In Malachi 3:10, when God speaks about the blessing He will pour out on your act of sowing, He does not limit it to financial provision. He simply says "blessing." And His blessings can include miracles such as healing and deliverance. What you sow you will reap (Gal. 6:7).

Never give to God as if He's a vending machine or treat the receiving of miracles as a transaction, however. It's also important to know that sowing is simply one way God releases miracles. The spiritual principle of sowing as a way of receiving miracles provides another vehicle by which God chooses to release His blessings.

When you sow into anointed ground at a true, anointed ministry, you will reap from that same ground. You will reap more anointing for whatever you need in your life spiritually and physically. Again, this is *one* of the ways God releases miracles. Do not get it twisted: you cannot buy miracles! This is a spiritual principle we are talking about, not a physical one. Your act of sowing into anointed ground is a spiritual principle of surrendering, sacrificing, seeking God, obeying God, and having faith.

When you give to the church, make sure you give spiritually rather than by religious tradition or by simply going through the motions. Seek the Holy Spirit, and ask Him what He wants you to give each time, instead of having a set amount that you just give without thinking. And give with intention. Be intentional to sacrifice and give generously. Be intentional at times to give purely out of thanksgiving to God. Be intentional to sow where you need a reaping. For example, if you need something such as financial provision or deliverance, sow a seed for that need. Sowing a seed in this way is like putting a tomato plant seed in the ground with the expectation that a tomato plant will come up and bear fruit.

When you sow, the seed does not go to waste. It will

produce a harvest. When you sow seeds of this kind, declare out loud the specific need you are sowing for, believing God for the harvest and thanking Him for fulfilling that need. Your seed is also a way of saying, "Thank You, God, in advance," as an action of faith that you believe God is releasing what you need and that you're grateful for the miracle He has on the way. Sowing is not necessary to receive deliverance. However, it is wise to sow with intention to thank God in advance, as well as to sow in a time of need, believing there will come a time of reaping.

THE KEYS OF THE KINGDOM

Most of those who have ministered deliverance for a long period of time will probably admit there have been some (or even many) cases in which they could not cast demons out of a person. Though they tried for many hours or sessions and with many "techniques," the person remained bound. The reason for this is that either (1) the minister did not have a high enough level of anointing to cast out the high-level demon (such as a demonic principality), or (2) the demonic oppression was complex and required a specific key to unlock the deliverance.

Remember, Peter was given the keys of the kingdom.

> I will give you the keys of the kingdom of heaven, and whatever you bind on earth will be bound in heaven, and whatever you loose on earth will be loosed in heaven.
> —MATTHEW 16:19, NKJV

Jesus did not give the keys to all the disciples. He entrusted Peter to both reveal the keys to the others and use the keys. Only those who are humble can understand the deeper revelations associated with these keys.

> At that time Jesus prayed this prayer: "O Father, Lord of heaven and earth, thank you for hiding these things from those who think themselves wise and clever, and for revealing them to the childlike."
> —MATTHEW 11:25, NLT

Jesus spoke this right after the disciples came back from casting out demons for the first time. When Jesus says "these things," He is referring to the keys (revelations) in the spiritual realm to unlock people from their demonic bondage. So be warned: if you do not humble yourself, you won't be able to comprehend these keys I'm sharing with you.

Part of having this revelation of the deeper things in the spiritual realm is understanding the proper use of certain keys. In some situations the basic keys of having faith, positioning oneself where the anointing is flowing, and renouncing sins are just not enough to make the demon flee. Sometimes another key is needed.

Jesus did not minister in the same way every time. He ministered according to what He saw prophetically. He determined which keys were needed to unlock a person's freedom and then directed the person a specific way. For instance, Jesus saw that faith was the key needed for Jairus' daughter to be healed, so He gave Jairus the prophetic direction "Don't be afraid; just believe" (Luke 8:50). When Jesus saw that the healing of the ten lepers would happen over time, as they walked out their faith and obeyed His word, He said to them, "Go, show yourselves to the priests," and on their way they were healed (17:14). Jesus could see that another leper should sow a financial seed to the house of God to receive and maintain his healing miracle. So, He instructed the leper to do just that:

> Then He put out His hand and touched him, saying, "I am willing; be cleansed." Immediately the leprosy left him. And He charged him to tell no one, "But go and show yourself to the priest, and make an offering for your cleansing, as a testimony to them, just as Moses commanded."
>
> —LUKE 5:13–14, NKJV

GOD MOVES UPON SACRIFICE

Another principle in the spiritual realm is that God moves upon sacrifice. Sacrifices move the heart of God. At times, a sacrifice is the key that unlocks the miracle.

This principle is found numerous times in Scripture. Many are familiar with the story of Solomon: God asked him what he desired, and Solomon asked for wisdom. But what they may not realize is why God was so moved to ask Solomon what he desired.

> The king went to Gibeon [near Jerusalem, where the tabernacle and the bronze altar stood] to sacrifice there, for that was the great high place. Solomon offered a thousand burnt offerings on that altar. In Gibeon the LORD appeared to Solomon in a dream at night; and God said, "Ask [Me] what I shall give you."
>
> —1 KINGS 3:4–5, AMP

Solomon brought a sacrifice, an offering. And after he did so, the Lord was moved to bless Solomon and give him what he desired.

> I will do what you have asked. I will give you a wise and discerning heart, so that there will never have been anyone like you, nor will there ever be. Moreover, I will give you what you have not asked for—both wealth and honor—so that in your lifetime you will have no equal among kings.
>
> —1 KINGS 3:12–13

He gave Solomon the blessing of not only wisdom but also wealth and honor, "a blessing until there {was} no more room to receive it" (Mal. 3:10, AMP).

God's hand was also moved upon David's sacrifice.

> Then Gad [the prophet] came to David that day and said to him, "Go up, set up an altar to the LORD on the threshing floor of Araunah the Jebusite [where you saw the angel]." So David went up according to Gad's word, as the LORD commanded. Araunah looked down and saw the king and his servants crossing over toward him; and he went out and bowed before the king with his face toward the ground. Araunah said, "Why has my lord the king come to his servant?" And David said, "To buy the threshing floor from you, to build an altar to the LORD, so that the plague may be held back from the people." Araunah said to David, "Let my lord the king take and offer up whatever seems good to him. Look, here are oxen for the burnt offering, and threshing sledges and the yokes of the oxen for the wood. All of this, O king, Araunah gives to

the king." And Araunah said to the king, "May the LORD your God be favorable to you." But the king said to Araunah, "No, but I will certainly buy it from you for a price. I will not offer burnt offerings to the LORD my God which cost me nothing." So David purchased the threshing floor and the oxen for fifty shekels of silver. David built an altar to the LORD there, and offered burnt offerings and peace offerings. So the LORD was moved [to compassion] by [David's] prayer for the land, and the plague was held back from Israel.

—2 SAMUEL 24:18–25, AMP

David sowed with intention for the plague to be lifted. He understood this principle of sowing and reaping. He grasped the principle that God's hand is moved by sacrifice. Araunah tried to donate the oxen to be used as David's sacrifice. But David knew the sacrifice needed to come from him personally for it to be true and acceptable to God. The Lord was moved by David's sacrifice, and He held back the plague from Israel.

In the time of Noah, after the rain had ceased and the ark docked on dry ground, Noah made a sacrifice to God.

Noah built an altar to the LORD, and took of every [ceremonially] clean animal and of every clean bird and offered burnt offerings on the altar. The LORD smelled the pleasing aroma [a soothing, satisfying scent] and the LORD said to Himself, "I will never again curse the ground because of man, for the intent (strong inclination, desire) of man's heart is wicked from his youth; and I will never again destroy every living thing, as I have done."

—GENESIS 8:20–21, AMP

Noah's sacrifice was a pleasing aroma to the Lord, meaning God was pleased by the sacrifice. This caused Him to speak this powerful covenant that He would never again destroy every living thing.

The more you surrender and obey God, the more rewards will come in your life. When you make sacrifices to God, they touch His heart, and He is moved to bring reward.

> As you know, you Philippians were the only ones who gave me financial help when I first brought you the Good News and then traveled on from Macedonia. No other church did this. Even when I was in Thessalonica you sent help more than once. I don't say this because I want a gift from you. Rather, I want you to receive a reward for your kindness.
>
> At the moment I have all I need—and more! I am generously supplied with the gifts you sent me with Epaphroditus. *They are a sweet-smelling sacrifice that is acceptable and pleasing to God.* And this same God who takes care of me will supply all your needs from his glorious riches, which have been given to us in Christ Jesus.
>
> —PHILIPPIANS 4:15–19, NLT, EMPHASIS ADDED

Just as the sacrifices made in the Old Covenant were a "sweet-smelling sacrifice" to the Lord, the same is true in the New Covenant. Many principles in the kingdom of God are found in both the Old and New Testaments. For example, the principle of impartation is demonstrated through Elijah and Elisha and is also seen through Jesus and the Twelve, as well as through Paul and Timothy. Likewise, the principle of a sacrifice moving the hand of God is demonstrated by Solomon and David and by the Philippians.

SOWING AS A KEY THAT UNLOCKS DELIVERANCE

When a person's demonic oppression is deep and complex, oftentimes making a sacrifice is one of the keys that unlocks the deliverance. A big reason for this has to do with the principle of sowing and reaping. If a person sows a lot into the kingdom of darkness, there's going to be a huge reaping. In most cases, that reaping does not automatically go away once a person repents.

As an example, if you mismanage money and are deeply in debt, say for a gambling or shopping addiction, once you receive Jesus as Lord, the debt does not automatically go away. God may do miracles and supernaturally erase some of it. But there are still repercussions to deal with. If you were cruel to your family in the past, they don't automatically forget those situations once you come to Jesus. You reaped distrust, and you must work to gain that trust back. If church leaders abuse their power, they don't get the opportunity to keep leading once they repent. There are repercussions. They've reaped distrust, and they have to work to prove that their repentance is genuine. They also need to put forth the spiritual work to be transformed more into God's image so they don't repeat abusive behavior. All of these may seem like physical examples, but they are indeed spiritual. All of them are related to spiritual sowing and reaping.

The same is true when one sows heavily into the devil's kingdom. If a witch or warlock has served the devil for years, they have sown deeply into the devil's kingdom—and a demonic spiritual reaping comes with that. The former warlock or witch, or perhaps someone who just wanted the devil to fulfill their desires, have made sacrifices to the devil's kingdom. The demonic oppression is more complex when a person willingly chooses to sow into the devil's kingdom.

Even if you've sown a great amount into the devil's kingdom, your deliverance process doesn't necessarily need to take a long time. Sometimes God delivers layer by layer over time, especially when the oppression is deep. But it's not as if you have to wait for time to take its toll as the demonic reaping is undone. Making a sacrifice or sacrifices to God's kingdom voids the sacrifices you made to the devil's kingdom. This is how it works in the spiritual realm.

If a person has demonic oppression because of negative words spoken over their life, then speaking words to break those curses unlocks the deliverance. When sacrifice (spiritual and financial) has been given to the devil, sacrifice to the kingdom of God unlocks the deliverance.

> Remember this: Whoever sows sparingly will also reap sparingly, and whoever sows generously will also reap generously.
> —2 CORINTHIANS 9:6

This scripture works for both kingdoms. If you sow generously into the devil's kingdom, you will also reap generously from it. Making sacrifices for the benefit of the kingdom of darkness is equivalent to willfully making a deep commitment to sow into and/or serve the devil's kingdom. To undo this in the spiritual realm, you need to make a sacrifice to God's kingdom to solidify and show with action the renouncing and repenting you are now doing.

It is not a matter of "Can't God see my heart, recognize

that my repentance is genuine, and just remove the demonic reaping?" It's a matter of spiritual principles and laws. God does not go against His principles. People can say, "Why do I have to go to the church and position myself where the anointing is flowing? Why can't I just pray to God directly so He can work the miracle right away?" God has His ways. He has His laws and principles in the spiritual realm. When you use your free will to choose to serve the devil and sow into his kingdom, the principle of undoing the reaping of those actions is to sow into God's kingdom and make a sacrifice to God. If you have contributed to the devil's kingdom, how much more should you desire to contribute to God's kingdom! There should be no question of "Why do I have to do this?"; rather, with true remorse, the fear of God, and love for God, you should desire to sacrifice greatly to God's kingdom.

When you come to Jesus in true repentance, He removes your past, your sins, and your oppression and sickness. But this occurs as you truly come to Jesus by following Him and obeying His commands. All that Jesus provides, including deliverance, is completely free. It can never be bought. Yet to receive all that Jesus provides, you have to follow both His Word and His principles. In the cases described in this section, that involves the act of making a sacrifice to God's kingdom.

The main examples of sowing into the devil's kingdom are doing witchcraft and seeking witchcraft, including things like visiting a psychic and paying them money to tell your fortune. Many people have testified that upon sowing into the kingdom of God via my ministry (5F Church), their deliverance took place. Many had already experienced deliverance from various things without sowing but found that one area of oppression kept remaining. Once they sowed based on that need, they reaped the anointing to destroy the yoke and were set free. Sowing was their key to deliverance for that specific bondage.

One of the most memorable testimonies of freedom upon sowing came from an event where I was ministering. As mass deliverance was occurring, I noticed a young boy manifesting on the ground; his mom told me she had taken him to many deliverance ministers, but no one could cast the demons out of her son. Every time, the boy continued to manifest, never being set free. After hearing testimonies of deliverance, she decided to travel with her son to attend this event. She had faith that this time God would deliver her son.

As I began to minister to the boy, I noticed prophetically that the oppression was complex. God revealed to me that the bondage had to do with generational sowing into the devil's kingdom. I asked the mom, "Have you ever sowed into the devil's kingdom—for example, given money to a psychic?"

She replied, "Yes, hundreds."

I then released prophetic direction as God revealed the key for her son's deliverance. I shared with her this key of making a sacrifice into God's kingdom. I did not tell her to sow anywhere specific or to my ministry but rather explained the importance of sowing into anointed ground because "what you sow into is what you will reap."

After explaining this, I began to pray for many others who were manifesting. About twenty minutes later, as I was in the middle of praying for someone, the mother came up to me and excitedly shared that her son had just been set free. She said that after the prophetic direction I released, she went to her phone and gave online to the ministry. Immediately after she sowed, her son began to cough. Demons left him! He was standing beside her totally set free!

The mother was overcome with gratitude, awe, and joy at what God had done. I'll never forget that moment. I was so grateful to God for releasing the keys of the kingdom that had been missing for this precious boy. It caused my faith to grow so big as to believe that anyone and everyone can be delivered and healed of anything, no matter how severe and complex the demonic oppression. When the anointing and the keys of the kingdom are present, any miracle can happen, and every demon must go!

A history of generational witchcraft is another example of where demonic oppression may be deep and complex. If one's parents or other family members in past generations have performed witchcraft, the devil often demands sacrifices be made for upcoming generations, such as sending curses on a future family member. In these cases, sowing into God's kingdom is often the key that unlocks the deliverance and voids the demonic reaping that came from past generations.

HOW TO SOW TO UNLOCK FREEDOM

If you're hearing from the Holy Spirit that the key for your deliverance is to sow into God's kingdom, it's important that you sow properly. First, make sure you sow into anointed ground. Ideally, you should be planted at a church where the leader is anointed and has fruits in their ministry of people being set free, healed, and transformed.

If you haven't yet discovered where God is calling you to be planted, or if you're currently attending a church that doesn't have the anointing to destroy yokes, ask God to help you identify where the "Peters" of today are. Find where the true anointing is, and sow there so you can reap from that ground and the yokes can be destroyed.

If you have sown a lot into the kingdom of darkness, then sow a lot into God's kingdom. You may need to sow over a period of time with continual seeds, not just one. Follow the Holy Spirit's voice and use the wisdom He's given you to discern what amount to sow.

If you're experiencing a lack of finances in this season, contribute in other ways, and make sacrifices to the kingdom of God by serving and helping advance His work. If you're unsure how to go about this, you can first serve God by spreading the news of what He's doing in the ministry where you're planted. Develop a heart to sow into God's kingdom, and He will open doors for you to receive provision so you have seeds to sow.

If our churches don't look like the Acts church and we aren't seeing the fruits of all being healed as Peter and Paul did, we are missing something. By and large, we have been missing the anointing, as well as many of the keys of the kingdom. The body of Christ has been missing the revelation of how to unlock people from cases of deep demonic oppression, so the oppressed have remained bound.

It's so important to humble yourself and receive these precious keys of the kingdom that God is releasing now in this revival we are living in. God's people must be free! May we never again turn a blind eye to people with tough cases of demonic oppression, rejecting them and forgetting about them. Instead, we must humble ourselves to receive the anointing and important keys of deliverance that have been absent in the body of Christ for far too long. The oppressed must be set free!

Chapter 10

ARE YOU READY TO BE FREE?

I BELIEVE THIS CHAPTER will be the most life-changing chapter you've ever read because through it you will receive deliverance, healing, and miracles. Keys have been released to unlock your deliverance *right now*. God has moved through so many vehicles—a shadow, aprons, handkerchiefs, a word spoken from afar—and in this revival I've seen Him deliver thousands of people through screens.

As I've commanded demonic spirits and sicknesses to go, countless people all over the world have immediately received deliverance. As I've declared from my church in Los Angeles that oppression and sickness must go, people in Australia, Asia, Europe, and South America have received freedom and healing. In every nation where I've ministered, miracles and deliverance have been released in the same way we've experienced at 5F Church.

God has revealed to me that just as He delivered people through their screens as they watched, He is now going to deliver you as you read these words. I advise you to designate time and a quiet, private space for this divine appointment with God that is about to take place. Make sure you have at least a few hours to allow God to work in you, to praise Him, and to spend time with Him.

If you have people around you, let them know you're about to receive deliverance and healing. Explain that they don't need to worry or start trying to cast demons out of you if you manifest. When deliverance occurs, manifestations may or may not accompany it. Deep oppression tends to result in more manifestations. These manifestations can sometimes involve a person shaking, crying, or coughing up spirits. Other spirits may scream as they leave a person.

It's best to come under the shadow of anointing without other people declaring and saying prayers over you during your deliverance. God's proper order is to have one specific leader ministering in their own spiritual dominion, not many people executing authority all at once. It's like you are coming under the apostle Peter's shadow right now (my shadow of anointing). Demonic spirits will obey and leave the most effectively when no one else is interfering.

Go into a room by yourself, or if you want other people around, make sure to explain the importance of not touching you or trying to cast demons out of you. It's crucial to just let the anointing come through the declarations stated below. Let these words do all the work in your deliverance. I recommend preparing to play my YouTube video called "Deliverance Prayer: Unlock Your Deliverance" (search on my YouTube page: youtube.com/apostlekathrynkrick). After reading the deliverance prayer in the next section, you may want to continue receiving prayer as you allow the anointing to flow to you through this video.

DELIVERANCE PRAYER

First, if you have any objects that may have demonic attachments, bring them into the room where you will receive deliverance. Also, place a trash bag or bin nearby. Next, bring out your renouncing list. If you haven't already, take as much time as you need with the Holy Spirit to recall and write down all you need to renounce.

Be still and take time to commune with the Holy Spirit. Renew your mind with the truth that Jesus is your Healer and Deliverer. He is so powerful, and nothing can limit Him. Renew your mind with the truth that Jesus wants you to be healed and delivered right now, because He's already paid the price for your deliverance. Remind yourself that this is your divine appointment with God to access and receive the inheritance that is yours as His child. Remind yourself that because you are coming in line with God's ways of releasing deliverance and healing, you indeed *will* receive miracles right now. The anointing flowing through these pages is so real, so powerful, and is truly Jesus Himself. Because of your faith, you must be healed and set free! Declare this out loud:

I believe that by Jesus' stripes I am healed. I believe in the power of His blood. I believe that as a child of God I have an inheritance that includes healing and freedom. I believe that Jesus wants to heal and deliver me and that it is going to happen today! I believe in God's anointing. I believe that the anointing flowing through this page will deliver and heal me now!

Now take a moment to surrender to Jesus. Jesus is the one delivering and healing you, and He doesn't force Himself.

He has filled the hungry with good things.
—Luke 1:53

Jesus fills the hungry, not the full. And He moves upon faith. The greater the faith, the more He will come. Remember, faith is not about a feeling. It's about choosing to believe. As you speak the Word of God despite how you feel, you demonstrate faith. Surrender to Jesus, allowing Him to come however He wants to heal and deliver you. Maybe you thought you needed one-on-one prayer to receive deliverance. Maybe you did not expect your deliverance to come through this book. It's important for you to tell God something like the following:

> *Lord, have Your way in my life. I know I need deliverance, and I desire deliverance. I desire Your will—that I would be set free and live an abundant life so I can shine the brightest for You to be glorified and the lost to be found. I surrender to Your ways of delivering me. I give You permission, and I desire for You to come through this page right now, in this room, and deliver me. I receive my healing and deliverance now.*

It's time to be set free!

If you have objects you need to renounce and discard, once you're ready, renounce these objects by speaking this aloud:

> *I renounce _____.*

> ***Apostle Kathryn Krick speaking:*** *I detach you from these objects and any demonic attachment connected to these items.*

Now throw away these objects.

Apostle Kathryn Krick speaking: I declare that every spirit attached to those objects must leave you now in Jesus' name. I declare that all spirits of witchcraft and manipulation must go. I declare that every curse associated with these objects must be broken off you now in Jesus' name. Any tie that was attaching you to another person through one of these objects must be broken now in Jesus' name!

Now it's time to be free from everything you have written down on your renouncing list and any other oppression on your life.

Once you're ready, begin renouncing by speaking aloud your list, such as "I renounce _____." Go ahead and renounce your entire list now. You can also renounce on behalf of your child, if your child needs deliverance.

Apostle Kathryn Krick speaking: I declare that your time for freedom is now! I break every generational curse off your life. I break every word curse and every curse of witchcraft sent upon you. I break every demonic soul tie. I cancel every demonic covenant. I detach you from everything you have renounced. I declare that every spirit attached must go from you now! Every spirit of witchcraft must go. Every spirit of death must go. Suicidal thoughts must go. The spirit of anxiety must go. Depression must go. Addiction must go. Demonic sexual spirits must go. Any spiritual spouse must go. Every spirit that torments you in the night must go. Spirits sending demonic dreams must go. Every spirit of mental illness must go.

Autism must go. Every spirit that speaks against your identity in Christ must go. The spirit of condemnation must go. The spirit of religion must go. Every spirit that entered through abuse must go. The spirit of poverty must go. The spirit of stagnancy must go. The spirit of rejection must go. The orphan spirit must go. Every spirit sending bombarding thoughts and every spirit sending demonic voices must go. Every spirit of body dysmorphia must go. OCD must go. I declare all spirits of infirmity must go. Every sickness, disease, and pain must go. Every problem in your body must leave. Every dead thing in your body must come alive! Whatever senses you have lost, they must be restored now. I declare eyes and ears to open. I declare creative miracles to wherever in your body there is something missing, from your mind to your entire body. I declare complete freedom and healing to you now in Jesus' name!

Praise God! I know He has just delivered you!

Thank You, Jesus, for Your power and Your love that has just come through these pages and touched Your child. Thank You, Jesus, for destroying the works of the devil! Thank You for bringing freedom and healing to Your child.

Take a moment to praise God right now with all your heart, mind, and strength.

Let all that I am praise the LORD; with my whole heart, I will praise his holy name. Let all that I am praise the Lord; may I never forget the good things he does for me. He forgives all my sins and heals all my diseases. He redeems me from death and crowns me with love and tender mercies. He fills my life with good things. My youth is renewed like the eagle's!

—Psalm 103:1–5, nlt

The demonic oppression has left, and now there is a void that the Holy Spirit wants to fill. God wants to fill you with His Spirit. If you've never received the baptism of the Holy Spirit, it's time to receive it *now*. If you already have, it's time to receive a fresh infilling of the Holy Spirit in your life.

The Baptism of the Holy Spirit

John answered their questions by saying, "I baptize you with water; but someone is coming soon who is greater than I am—so much greater that I'm not even worthy to be his slave and untie the straps of his sandals. He will baptize you with the Holy Spirit and with fire."

—Luke 3:16, nlt

The baptism of the Holy Spirit is a baptism of fire. It's a powerful measure of the Holy Spirit that comes into your life for the purpose of strengthening your spirit to help you live by the Spirit. It's an infilling of the Holy Spirit that is like fire in the spiritual realm—it energizes you spiritually and physically and makes you joyful. The more spiritual you are, the more joyful, full of faith, and in love with Jesus you will be. The baptism of the Holy Spirit is a force that sets your spirit ablaze to help you become more spiritual.

This baptism is typically a separate occurrence from and of a greater measure than the infilling of the Holy Spirit that comes at one's salvation. A big reason for this is that the baptism of the Holy Spirit usually comes when a person is ready to surrender fully to God. Upon salvation, many times a person isn't quite sure about surrendering everything but simply believes that Jesus is Lord and wants to begin following Him. Therefore, the baptism of the Holy Spirit is a secondary infilling. There can be instances, however, when someone receives the Holy Spirit upon giving their life to Jesus and simultaneously is baptized in the Holy Spirit.

Many do not know about the baptism of the Holy Spirit and are missing out on so much of His presence and the gift of tongues. Yet this baptism is clearly explained in the Word of God:

> You will receive power when the Holy Spirit comes upon you. And you will be my witnesses, telling people about me everywhere—in Jerusalem, throughout Judea, in Samaria, and to the ends of the earth.
>
> —ACTS 1:8, NLT

The Holy Spirit coming *upon* speaks of the baptism of the Holy Spirit—the fire coming on a believer.

> On the day of Pentecost all the believers were meeting together in one place. Suddenly, there was a sound from heaven like the roaring of a mighty windstorm, and it filled the house where they were sitting. Then, what looked like flames or tongues

> of fire appeared and settled on each of them. And
> everyone present was filled with the Holy Spirit
> and began speaking in other languages, as the Holy
> Spirit gave them this ability.
>
> —ACTS 2:1–4, NLT

The term *tongues of fire* speaks of the Holy Spirit coming in fire. All the believers received the gift of tongues. The ability to speak in tongues and the baptism of the Holy Spirit are gifts that God wants to give all His children. They are necessary to be strong spiritually and live completely by the Spirit.

> Even as Peter was saying these things, the Holy Spirit
> fell upon all who were listening to the message. The
> Jewish believers who came with Peter were amazed
> that the gift of the Holy Spirit had been poured out
> on the Gentiles, too. For they heard them speaking
> in other tongues and praising God.
>
> —ACTS 10:44–46, NLT

As Peter was preaching, the Holy Spirit fell *upon* the people, and they began speaking in tongues. One way to receive the baptism of the Holy Spirit is for an anointed servant of God to speak the words over a person, such as "Be baptized in the Holy Spirit." The Holy Spirit then comes in fire upon the person.

Also, just being in the presence of the anointing can cause the Holy Spirit to come in fire upon people. When I minister, often after a person has been delivered, God will soon release His Spirit upon them. The person begins speaking in tongues without me laying hands on them or saying, "I release the baptism of the Holy Spirit to you."

Another way the baptism of the Holy Spirit comes, which I just alluded to, is by the laying on of hands:

> As soon as they heard this, they were baptized in the name of the Lord Jesus. Then when Paul laid his hands on them, the Holy Spirit came on them, and they spoke in other tongues and prophesied.
>
> —ACTS 19:5–6, NLT

This scripture also shows that there are two different baptisms: water baptism and the baptism of the Holy Spirit.

A key to receiving the baptism of the Holy Spirit is to surrender everything to Jesus. I have been a believer every day of my life that I can remember. My first memory is of accepting Jesus as my Lord at age four. But I didn't encounter the Holy Spirit coming in power until my mid-twenties. When I encountered God's power, it was like I truly met Jesus rather than just hearing about Him and believing in Him. Once I met Him, my eyes opened to His indescribable love for the first time.

All of a sudden, I had a knowing that God was always with me and knew me intimately. I had a knowing that He has never condemned me and that His thoughts for me have always been good. I had a knowing that His future plans for me are so good. I believed in all these things before, but now I *knew* they were true, and I believed them with all my heart.

Meeting Jesus led me to fall in love with Him. And from there I was moved to surrender everything for the first time. Once I surrendered to God and desired for His Spirit to overtake me and have His way, the baptism of the Holy Spirit came. I immediately erupted in speaking in tongues and was full of the fire of the Holy Spirit. The baptism of the Holy Spirit came *when* I surrendered to God and desired Him to have His way. The gift of tongues comes with the baptism of the Holy Spirit. For some, it may not manifest immediately, but the gift has been released. As you draw closer to God and become more surrendered, the gift of tongues will be activated and manifest.

> He who speaks in a tongue edifies himself.
> —1 Corinthians 14:4, nkjv

Speaking in tongues is both a gift and a tool from God to help strengthen your spirit and push down your carnal nature. So the baptism of the Holy Spirit is for those who truly do not want to live lukewarm lives anymore and don't want any part of their carnal nature. The baptism of the Holy Spirit releases the fire of the Holy Spirit and tongues, which consumes the carnal man when invited to. This means if you yield to the Holy Spirit, cherish Him, and value the gift of tongues, the Holy Spirit will powerfully take over your life.

When I received the fire of the Holy Spirit, I embraced Him fully. I desired my life to be in God's will every step, every day. I no longer desired the things of this world. I felt fire spiritually. I felt so much uncontainable joy and energy like never before in my life. I yearned to spend time with Jesus more than ever before. I strongly desired to do things that pleased Jesus only. The Holy Spirit is the One who gave me those desires through His precious fire. I said "Yes and amen" to the new me. I kept leaning into the Holy Spirit and following Him in this new life of being totally surrendered and on fire for Him.

The baptism of the Holy Spirit comes when He is

valued and used in your life. This baptism does not come haphazardly, and it is not to be wasted. When you're ready for the all-consuming fire to envelop your life, the Holy Spirit will come!

If you have never surrendered your entire life, surrender to God now! Speak your surrender from your heart. Tell God that you want His will completely, even if it means sacrificing your dreams for His. Tell Him you desire and are ready for Him to baptize you with His Spirit.

> *Apostle Kathryn Krick speaking: I release the baptism of the Holy Spirit to come upon you now. May the fire of the Holy Spirit fill you to over-flowing now in Jesus' name! Be filled with peace and joy, and may God's love envelop you! May you be set on fire for Jesus from now on! May your heart be ablaze every day for Jesus. May the fear of God come upon you, helping you to always stay in His will and please Him. May this fire for Jesus grow bigger every day!*

Open your mouth and praise God with your words. Allow God to overtake every part of you, including your tongue. Spend time in His presence and pray in the Spirit.

> *Thank You, Jesus, for what You have just done. Thank You for doing miracles. Thank You for Your precious and powerful Spirit. Thank You for releasing more of Your Spirit and filling the hungry!*

I encourage you to read the next three chapters in a timely manner, without letting too much time pass. In these chapters you will learn how to maintain your deliverance. Since you've just been set free, it's important that you immediately be equipped to know the enemy's schemes. When you are aware of the enemy's tactics, you will be able to walk in victory over his evil strategies and maintain your freedom.

MAINTAINING YOUR DELIVERANCE: SURRENDER

*I*F YOU NEEDED deliverance prior to reading this book, I believe God's power has set you free as you read. Every person's spiritual case is different. Some who read this book may receive complete deliverance. Others of you may have more complex oppression, and/or God wants to deliver you layer by layer.

Why does God deliver layer by layer at times? It has to do with the wisdom and sovereignty of God. Often, in His wisdom He knows that if He brings total deliverance immediately, before one has fully surrendered and been transformed, the person may give in to the enemy's traps and go back into the world, not taking God seriously. They may disvalue what Jesus did and treat their deliverance as a hospital visit or quick fix rather than change their lifestyle and surrender everything to Jesus.

At other times, God delivers layer by layer simply because He decides to do it that way. If you have been delivered of some oppression but there are more layers left, I encourage you to tune into my live streams and posted videos on my YouTube channel. As you keep positioning yourself where the anointing is flowing, God will continue to deliver you layer by layer. In addition, I encourage you to attend an event, conference, or Sunday service at

5F Church. Go to 5fchurch.org or apostlekathrynkrick.com for all the details.

Now that you've been set free, you must do something very important: maintain your deliverance. This is not a onetime task but a lifestyle. If you value your freedom and want to remain free, you must take maintaining your deliverance very seriously.

> When an impure spirit comes out of a person, it goes through arid places seeking rest and does not find it. Then it says, "I will return to the house I left." When it arrives, it finds the house unoccupied, swept clean and put in order. Then it goes and takes with it seven other spirits more wicked than itself, and they go in and live there. And the final condition of that person is worse than the first. That is how it will be with this wicked generation.
>
> —MATTHEW 12:43–45

The devil is completely evil. He has no grace or mercy in him. He wants to steal, kill, and destroy and is no respecter of persons. He wants to bring torment to the old and young alike. One day we will live in heaven where the devil is not. But for now we live on this earth where the enemy is the "prince of the power of the air" (Eph. 2:2, AMP), or as it is written in The Passion Translation:

> It wasn't that long ago that you lived in the religion, customs, and values of this world, obeying the dark ruler of the earthly realm who fills the atmosphere with his authority, and works diligently in the hearts of those who are disobedient to the truth of God.
>
> —EPHESIANS 2:2

As long as we live on this earth, we must show up each day and fight the good fight of faith against the "dark ruler of the earthly realm" (Satan). With God's help we will always and easily be victorious. But we must do our part by obeying God and remaining surrendered. The more you walk in obedience to God, the stronger you become spiritually and the more the devil sees that attacking you is a waste of time. The more you obey God, the more you will receive the reward of the devil being unable to attack as much as he has in the past. As you increase in your obedience, your favor and protection also increase.

Imagine the land where you were in bondage is a place called Egypt. Now imagine your moment of freedom when you set sail from the shores of Egypt. The promised land (of total abundant life) is a boat ride away. If you've ever been on a boat, you know that when you first leave the shore, you can still hear the sounds of the city and see the city lights. So, as you first set sail, even though you're no longer in the land of Egypt, you're still very close. The farther you sail, the quieter its noises and the dimmer its lights become. Eventually you'll lose sight and sound of the land.

This is how it is in the spiritual realm. When you first leave the land of bondage, the enemy sees you as an easy target, at arm's length. Also, once you have been set free, the enemy is very angry at his loss. He tends to put more effort into those who are more likely to give in to his traps. He knows that those who are strong in the Lord and have increased favor are a waste of his time, because when he brings temptation, they keep resisting him in obedience to God. That's not to say he doesn't still attack the spiritually strong and those who've been in obedience for a long time. But it's more like how it ended

147

up with Jesus—the devil tempted Jesus in the wilderness and then "left him until an opportune time" (Luke 4:13). On the other hand, the enemy tends to attack those who are "close to Egypt" more frequently. This is the expanded revelation of Matthew 12:43–45.

Demons come from the devil and are in unity with him. They carry out their jobs based on the devil's instructions. When a demon is cast out, it has failed in its job, and punishment awaits it. The demon wants to come back to the person it lived in and, in revenge, bring more demons with it. When a person is set free, the demon's aim is to return with even more oppression. But if you take maintaining your deliverance seriously, no demon can ever come back! Even though the devil may try because you're not far from "Egypt," he is powerless when you have God on your side. And if you take maintaining your deliverance seriously, God will defeat the devil every single time he tries to attack.

So if you have just been delivered, there is absolutely nothing to fear. However, it's critical that you have the fear of God like never before. Now is not the time to be lazy in your faith. You have to be a committed child of God and soldier of Jesus. This should be basic Christianity. But in today's time where lukewarm Christianity is common and many in the body of Christ lack the fear of God, I must stress the importance of being a serious disciple who fears God.

One reason the devil so desires to bring back oppression is that when you were set free, it was a big loss for his kingdom. A part of his kingdom was destroyed and defeated when those chains broke! The second reason he wants to bring oppression back is that he wants to discredit the anointed servants of God. He wants people to think that deliverance isn't actually happening at the ministry where you were delivered. He wants to deceive people into thinking that deliverance is witchcraft or a setup involving actors.

The biggest scheme the devil has toward anointed ministers and their ministries is influencing people to think these ministries are fake by spewing lies through skeptics and Pharisees of today. The devil wants people who came to an anointed ministry to appear more bound than before. He wants to make the oppression even worse, hoping a bad testimony will be spoken. The attacks on recently delivered people are also attacks on the true servants of God, their ministries, and the whole kingdom of God.

Again, you must take maintaining your deliverance seriously, seeing it as a huge responsibility. When a minister casts a demon out of you, the minister does not have the responsibility to make sure you maintain your deliverance. Only you can do that. Ministers do have a responsibility of offering teaching and equipping that form you into a mature disciple who can walk in victory. But it's up to you to listen to or read the teachings. And it's your responsibility to value and actually apply the teachings. It's up to you to live a life of surrender to Jesus.

So that you'll be equipped to be victorious in every situation, the next three chapters will reveal the devil's schemes in bringing back oppression.

SURRENDER

The most important way to maintain your deliverance is through surrender to Jesus—yielding everything about your life to His authority and power. In fact, every other aspect of maintaining your deliverance builds on the foundation of surrender. "If you try to hang on to your life, you will lose it. But if you give up your life for my sake, you will save it" (Matt. 16:25, NLT).

If you do not surrender everything to Jesus, there is no way you can have victory over the devil. You will lose your freedom and lose a life of heaven on earth with Jesus. But if you give up your life to follow Jesus every single day, you will save your life. You will be saved from the enemy's grip. When you do not surrender to Jesus, you disable God's help. A 90 percent surrendered life is not good enough. It's like having most of the doors in your house locked but keeping one unlocked.

Surrendering everything to Jesus is the best decision you can make. It is definitely the best decision I've ever made. I agree with the apostle Paul completely when he says,

> I once thought these things were valuable, but now I consider them worthless because of what Christ has done. Yes, everything else is worthless when compared with the infinite value of knowing Christ Jesus my Lord. For his sake I have discarded everything else, counting it all as garbage, so that I could gain Christ.
> —PHILIPPIANS 3:7–8, NLT

Everything I've had to give up to follow Jesus has been completely worth it. The dreams I gave up for God, even if they were good dreams, were not in God's will for my life. And whatever is outside God's will is garbage. I do not want it! The worldly life of pleasures is no longer enticing when you taste the love of Jesus, the only One who brings true contentment, peace, and joy.

Living in relationship with God and walking in His will are the greatest pleasures in the entire universe. *Nothing* compares. The devil really has people fooled. If people would just recognize how the devil has deceived them, most would gladly give up their worldly lifestyles to follow Jesus. If you are hesitant to surrender everything to Jesus, I urge you to anyway. You will never regret it.

Those of you who really do not want to give up something—whether it's worldly friends, alcohol, partying, sex outside marriage, selfishness, or watching and listening to dark movies and music—I strongly encourage you to reconsider. All these things of the world are not worth it. The desire you feel to participate in these activities is coming from the enemy. He is influencing your feelings and thoughts. He's the father of lies, and he's lying to you, telling you, "It's no big deal. It's harmless." He's lying to you when he influences you to feel like this thing you're doing or engaging in is a source of great happiness.

All these temptations from the enemy are open doors when acted on. The fleshly pleasure of these things is not worth the demonic oppression that will come with it. Furthermore, these pleasures are not worth the condemning thoughts the devil will fill you with for not being obedient to Jesus. I once was blind to this, but now I see.

I wish I could tell my teenage self these things. I speak them to you with the love of God, as if you're my children. I feel God's heart for you so strongly as I write. God wants you to be safe in His arms. He wants intimacy and relationship with you. He wants to pour out so many blessings on you that there is no room for them all. He wants you to fulfill your purpose on this earth, and He wants to change the world through you. He wants to save souls and destroy the devil's grip in people's lives through you.

This is the *best* life. This most precious "heaven on earth" life can be found only when you surrender your entire life to Jesus. I do not promise what I cannot guarantee, and I truly *promise* you this. You cannot find contentment outside surrender to Jesus. This I am sure of. You were created with a void that only Jesus can fill. That void causes you to seek after love and contentment. It causes you to seek after purpose. When you surrender to Jesus, only then will that void be filled. You will experience the *greatest* love, contentment, and purpose. If you haven't already, now is the time to surrender every single part of your life to Jesus. Take a moment to be with Jesus and surrender to Him now.

SHUT ALL DOORS

> Do not give the devil a foothold.
> —EPHESIANS 4:27

Technically, when a person sins, they are opening the door. When they persist in sin, the door is opened wider. It is not just the obvious worldly acts that are sins. Sin is any action that goes against God's commands in the Bible and in His *rhema* word (His present-tense spoken word through servants of God). Sin can also include inaction to God's commands. To not spend time regularly in the Word of God is a sin. To keep the wrong friends (those who are not surrendered to God) close is a sin. (This does not include unsurrendered family members you are obliged to live with in this season of your life.) To speak careless negative words is a sin. To disrespect your spiritual leader is a sin. It is important for you to understand what is considered sin so you can also identify what exactly can open a door to the enemy.

If you do make a mistake and sin, intentionally or not, it doesn't mean that a demon automatically comes in. You should not live in paranoia that you can never make a mistake. God's grace is there to cover you. The spiritual danger of a sin lies in your continual return to that sin without genuine repentance. Sin is especially destructive when you live without the fear of God and treat obedience to God as something casual and optional.

> The temptations in your life are no different from what others experience. And God is faithful. He will not allow the temptation to be more than you can stand. When you are tempted, he will show you a way out so that you can endure.
> —1 CORINTHIANS 10:13, NLT

This scripture does not say God will not allow the temptation to be more than you can stand *some* of the time or *most* of the time. It says He won't allow this, period—full stop. In every circumstance God is faithful and will not allow the temptation to be beyond your ability to withstand. In every situation where you are tempted, He *will* show you a way out so you can endure. The key is surrender. That is what activates God's help, showing you a way out.

Many times, shutting the open door is what leads to deliverance. Shutting the door is the action of transferring whom you give your authority to—from the enemy to God. Once you're delivered, it's crucial that you keep those doors shut. Sometimes, by God's grace, He may deliver you before you've shut doors. If that is the case, it is very important for you to immediately shut those doors. If you were delivered from an addiction, get rid of the drugs, alcohol, porn, etc. If following certain people online causes you to be tempted to sin, unfollow them.

If you have close friends who have not surrendered to God, it is essential that you cut ties or put up boundaries depending on how the Holy Spirit is leading.

Keeping the wrong people close is a huge open door to the enemy. This is one of the biggest ways the devil tricks people, especially Christians. Christians justify having the wrong people close by telling themselves they're loving the individuals and being a light to them. Yet Jesus kept only twelve disciples semi-close to Him, and they were all surrendered to God. He then brought very close three disciples who were the most surrendered to God. Jesus chose to bring James, John, and Peter with Him in intimate and vulnerable moments, such as on the Mount of Transfiguration and in the Garden of Gethsemane (Matt. 17:1–13; 26:36–38). We are to follow Jesus' example for our spiritual safety.

"Do not be deceived: 'Bad company corrupts good morals'" (1 Cor. 15:33, AMP). To keep someone in close relationship while that person has open doors to the enemy is giving the enemy authority to speak through this person to you. The person's behavior alone will affect you and rub off on you because of this principle. No matter how hard you try, the person will corrupt your good morals, and oppression from the enemy can come.

This concept excludes family members you are obliged to live with. In these situations a special grace covers you since their proximity to you is out of your control. God will use whatever attack the enemy tries to bring through these family members as a refining fire to strengthen your faith and mold you more into His image. However, you need to understand the seriousness of being vigilant to fight the good fight of faith and continue the spiritual disciplines that keep you strong spiritually. We are all called to be on alert in the spiritual war we are in, but you must be *extra* vigilant, knowing your unique situation and understanding that it can be used as a refining fire.

Another important door you must close is that of negative speech. For some, this may be a complete lifestyle shift.

To be sure you're never opening doors with the words you say, resolve every morning to speak only words of life for the day. Resolve to think before you speak. Change does not come without intention. You must make the decision to change in this area. As you speak with intention day by day, eventually you will transform to be more like Jesus in your speech. Cursing and negative words will be eliminated from your language.

FILL YOURSELF WITH THE HOLY SPIRIT

Let's take another look at this scripture:

> When an impure spirit comes out of a person, it goes through arid places seeking rest and does not find it. Then it says, "I will return to the house I left." When it arrives, it finds the house unoccupied, swept clean and put in order. Then it goes and takes with it seven other spirits more wicked than itself, and they go in and live there. And the final condition of that person is worse than the first. That is how it will be with this wicked generation.
> —MATTHEW 12:43–45

Finding the house "unoccupied, swept clean and put in order" means the demon found the person void of the Holy Spirit. When a demon leaves, there is a void that must be filled with the Holy Spirit or a demon will see it has the authority to return. Filling yourself with the Holy Spirit is not a onetime occurrence but must involve actions you take daily.

> Do not get drunk on wine, which leads to debauchery. Instead, be filled with the Spirit, speaking to one another with psalms, hymns, and songs from the Spirit.
> —EPHESIANS 5:18–19

Now let's look at what it means to be filled with the Holy Spirit:

1. Surrender to the Holy Spirit, and allow Him to have His way, filling you and baptizing you with His Spirit. As I shared in chapter 10, the baptism of the Holy Spirit is crucial for a believer to live a life led by the Spirit and for their spirit to be stronger than their carnal nature. Receiving the fire of the Holy Spirit that comes with the baptism gives you the strength and power to resist the devil and crucify your flesh.

2. Enter into a relationship with God. This is not only a choice but also a discipline. If your relationship with God is based on feelings, it will be very fickle. Your relationship with God should be based on faith, as that is what everything in the kingdom is founded on. A young adult may not want to spend much time with their parents. They may desire to spend time with friends or be alone instead. Yet when the grown-up child *chooses* to spend time with their mom and dad, it's *because of their love* for their parents.

There may be days when you don't feel like spending time praying or reading the Word. That does not mean you don't love God or should be ashamed. It's important to understand that your relationship with God is not based on feelings but is based on your daily choice to love God. Otherwise, you'll neglect your relationship with God, and/or you'll believe the devil's lies of condemnation every time you don't feel like spending time in the Word or in prayer.

WHAT IS A RELATIONSHIP WITH GOD?

A relationship with God is made up of prayer, Scripture reading, worship, and obedience. All of these are based on choice and action, not on feelings.

Prayer

Many Christians do not actually know how to pray. They think they must pray alone in their room for many hours, with KJV language or other words that are unnatural to their vocabulary. Many also believe that prayer rituals and religious words persuade God to hear them and move on their behalf.

Prayer should come from a genuine relationship with God where there is real intimacy. Praying to God as if He's an unrelatable figure in a faraway land who doesn't understand your natural way of speaking does not constitute a relationship or intimacy. Having a relationship with God is choosing to make God your best friend, Father, and Lord all at the same time.

At times you should speak to God as you speak to your best friend: sharing many details throughout the day in your normal way of speaking and with respect, love, and vulnerability. You should consciously and intentionally bring God with you everywhere you go, every day. Create intimacy by renewing your mind that God is with you always.

Bring Him into your thoughts. When you see a gorgeous sunset, thank Him! When you experience His favor, thank Him! When your heart is blessed, thank Him!

When you are pondering His promises, tell Him,

> *Thank You, Lord, for the promises that will come to pass. I trust You. I trust Your timing. I thank You for taking me through all that I've gone through. You know the best way to transform me and refine me. I love You, Jesus.*

When you're passing through difficult times, say to Him,

> *Lord, I need Your help. Thank You that You are fighting my battles for me and helping me get through this. I know You have a purpose in every-thing You allow me to go through. Thank You, Lord, for being with me and helping me through this.*

Though God wants you to treat Him as your best friend, it doesn't mean He wants you to rattle off whatever you feel. There's power in your words, even when speaking to God. God wants you to live by faith, not feelings. It is by faith that we please God, not by venting our feelings. One way to show God you love Him is to obey Him, choosing to be spiritually mature and speaking only words that align with His Word. Treat God as your best friend but in a spiritually mature way, rather than perhaps your default way of speaking however you feel.

God also wants you to speak to Him as your Father and Lord. Always speak to Him with respect. When you treat Him as your best friend, make sure you also remember that He is your Father and Lord as well.

Another aspect of prayer is partnering with God to bring about His will on earth. You are called to walk in authority on this earth. You are called to heal the sick, cast out demons, and move mountains. This is all done with God's power as we partner with Him. But He calls us to take the authority and speak the Word. Many believers are praying wrongly, and that's why they aren't seeing results. They're praying, "God, please heal this person," when the proper way to pray is to declare "Be healed" or to command demons to go—that is, when it is in your spiritual domain and in order, led by the Holy Spirit.

> I assure you and most solemnly say to you, whoever says to this mountain, "Be lifted up and thrown into the sea!" and does not doubt in his heart [in God's unlimited power], but believes that what he says is going to take place, it will be done for him [in accordance with God's will].
>
> —MARK 11:23, AMP

Much of your prayer requests should instead be declaration words speaking to the mountain. As you declare, you are not acting alone. This is prayer. This is partnership with God to bring about His will.

Also, when you pray, you don't need to repeat your requests over and over until they come to pass. To repeat prayer requests shows a lack of faith that God has heard you. It's better to declare once and from there thank God for the miracle that is on its way.

If you're planted at a church where God's power is moving, prayers will be released to you during the services too. Those words cannot return void. God desires you to pray with understanding and faith. When you haven't yet seen the miracle manifest but are planted at an anointed church, thank God for the miracle that was released to you through the declarations (prayers) of the servant of God, and have faith that the miracle will be evident in His timing. It's important to receive what God has released through the servant of God rather than act like the prayers didn't happen just because you haven't seen the miracle manifest yet.

There is also a time to humbly present your requests to God. When you're asking God for direction and are unsure of His will and timing, give Him the authority. Come to God as a child, and share the pure desires of your heart with Him.

> You don't have what you want because you don't ask God for it. And even when you ask, you don't get it because your motives are all wrong—you want only what will give you pleasure.
>
> —James 4:2–3, NLT

Asking things of God should be done in a respectful way—not in selfishness but with pure motives. If you realize you want something for a selfish reason, ask God to help you become humbler and more selfless.

Saying "thank You" to God should be your most prevalent kind of prayer. This is how you "pray without ceasing" (1 Thess. 5:17–18, ESV). Many people think praying without ceasing means constantly bringing prayer requests to God, and some may feel insecure in their relationship with God because they run out of things to ask Him for after a few minutes. But if you're constantly asking God for things, either you're not trusting that He heard you or you're desiring way too many things and need to be more selfless.

If you don't have a great number of requests, that's a good thing, not a bad thing. It means you're trusting that God is working and content with His timing in bringing about the miracles. You're more focused on serving God and showing love to others than on all the things you don't have.

If you go on vacation with a friend or loved one, there will probably be times of silence between you. There is nothing wrong with that—it's intimacy nonetheless, even when no words are exchanged. That is how it is with Jesus. A main part of your relationship with God will be including Him in your heart, mind, and prayer wherever you go and thanking Him continually.

A relationship with God is not supposed to be complicated. However, religion tends to make everything complicated. The enemy's scheme through the spirit of religion tries to make everything in the kingdom of God seem unattainable. It's time to break free from that spirit of religion and enter into your precious and intimate relationship with God. You can start right now!

Reading the Word

> In the beginning was the Word, and the Word was with God, and the Word was God.
>
> —JOHN 1:1, NKJV

God *is* the Word. If you do not read the Word, you are not truly entering into a relationship with God. The Word reveals God's character. In the Word, God speaks. When you read the Word, you get to know God. You get to know His heart and His qualities such as faithfulness, goodness, purity, and indescribable love. The more you read the Word, the more you will know Him. The more you read the Word, the more you will know what His voice sounds like and will be able to hear that still, small voice guiding you, correcting you, and speaking to you each day. The more you read the Word, the more you'll be able to discern between the devil's voice and God's voice. Reading the Word is a big part of spending time with God and listening to Him.

Keep in mind, however, that the Pharisees and Jesus read the same Word of God, but their interpretations were completely different. The Pharisees' "revelation" of God's heart and His ways, as well as how to follow His commands, was in many ways opposite of Jesus'. So how do you make sure you're getting the true revelation—God's new wine and Jesus' revelation—rather than the Pharisees' version? You must be discipled.

> Therefore go and make disciples of all nations, baptizing them in the name of the Father and of the Son and of the Holy Spirit, and teaching them to obey everything I have commanded you. And surely I am with you always, to the very end of the age.
> —MATTHEW 28:19–20

You are called to be a *disciple*, and that means you must be discipled. Part of being discipled involves being taught and equipped by an anointed fivefold minister. Most of this teaching and equipping will come from your spiritual mother or father. According to Matthew 28:20, Jesus has sent anointed servants of God to guide you and teach you what God has commanded. Fivefold ministers are anointed to teach with true, new-wine revelation the meaning of the Scriptures. As you receive these teachings, anointing is imparted to you and helps you hear God's voice as you read His Word.

For example, you may have been taught wrongly that God wants you to follow His commands "just because." In this situation you will most likely read the Word as a set of laws you're forced to follow. But when you are taught properly that God has given you His Word as a road map to abundant life and a battle plan for victory over the devil, you'll read the Word with reverence, excitement, and joy! You'll take the words to heart, and you'll feel motivated to follow the commands.

If what you are taught wrongly doesn't share God's heart of grace, mercy, and compassion, you'll read the Word through the lens of condemnation. You'll feel that it's too difficult to do all God is asking you to do. However, if you have an anointed teacher who brings revelation of God's love, you'll read the Word as a love letter to you, recognizing God's love through what He is speaking in His Word.

Above all, you need the Holy Spirit to help you receive the proper revelation of God's Word. Part of accessing the Holy Spirit's help in this is by planting yourself under your God-appointed spiritual mother or father and continually surrendering to the Holy Spirit as you invite Him to have His way in your life.

> Therefore, get rid of all moral filth and the evil that is so prevalent and humbly accept the word planted in you, which can save you.
>
> Do not merely listen to the word, and so deceive yourselves. Do what it says. Anyone who listens to the word but does not do what it says is like someone who looks at his face in a mirror and, after looking at himself, goes away and immediately forgets what

he looks like. But whoever looks intently into the perfect law that gives freedom, and continues in it— not forgetting what they have heard, but doing it— they will be blessed in what they do.

—James 1:21–25

Getting the Word of God planted in you happens when you read it daily *and* when you are planted in an anointed ministry under the leadership of your spiritual mother or father. Some people get lazy in their own spiritual walks when they're in anointed churches, thinking that all they need to do is just show up to church and listen to the teachings. Yet listening to the Word through teachings and reading the Word of God oneself are equally important.

You need to have your own relationship with God and spend time with Him in the Word. Something very powerful and supernatural takes place as you do this, helping you not only have victory over the enemy but also maintain your deliverance.

As for how much of the Word you should read daily, be led by the Holy Spirit. Reading the Word should be a discipline, but don't let it turn into religion (an old-wine ritual). A general guideline is to make a habit of reading at least one chapter of the Word per day. But if you read only one verse on a particular day because of unusual busyness, it's not a huge deal. You should not feel condemnation for not finding time to read a whole chapter. Above all, spending time in the Word should be one of the main priorities of your day. It's important to live in God's grace while also having the fear of God. Be disciplined in reading the Word, but don't be religious about it. Make sure you give the Holy Spirit room to lead you in terms of what to read and how much to read.

If you are a new believer, it's good to start with the Book of John. If you are recently delivered, even if you've been a believer for a long time, be humble enough to see yourself as a young, newly free believer who is just beginning to experience the new wine.

Planting the Word in yourself and living out what the Word says are two of the most important ways to maintain your deliverance. The main reason people struggle to move forward after being set free or become oppressed again is that they are not filling themselves with the Word and applying it. Again, filling yourself with the Word can be accomplished by both reading it and listening to it through anointed teachings. James 1:21 says *the Word can save you!* Every day, look intently on the Word that truly brings freedom. Apply that Word to your life day after day and you will be blessed, living a life of continual victory over the devil and maintaining your freedom forever!

Worship

> Speaking to one another with psalms, hymns, and songs from the Spirit. Sing and make music from your heart to the Lord.
>
> —Ephesians 5:19

It is important to exalt God above everything else. In your relationship with God as your Lord, you should regularly praise Him and treat Him as the Lord of lords that He is. This worship can take place through many different means of expressing your adoration and praise, including through singing and dance and through your words. Worship can also be done through every aspect of your life. Everything you do should be done unto the Lord. "Whatever you do, work at it with all your heart, as working for the Lord, not for human masters" (Col. 3:23).

When you go to work, work with excellence and diligence. Treat everyone in your workplace with respect and love. Arrive on time, and be responsible and honest. Whether taking care of your children, caring for your physical body, cleaning your house—whatever you're doing—do it with excellence and to the best of your ability. As you do all these things with the purpose of obeying God, you are worshipping Him. Everything He is asking you to do, do as worship unto Him—not because He's "forcing" you to but because you revere Him and want to obey Him. Do it all with excellence because He is Lord and knows best.

Obedience

I like to describe obedience as God's "love language," meaning that obeying God is what touches His heart the most. Many people wrongly think that religious rituals such as praying repetitive or impassioned prayers, fasting routinely out of tradition, and so forth, are spiritually impressive to God or are the way to His heart.

> But Samuel replied, "What is more pleasing to the LORD: your burnt offerings and sacrifices or your obedience to his voice? Listen! Obedience is better than sacrifice, and submission is better than offering the fat of rams.
> —1 SAMUEL 15:22, NLT

Saul thought that making religious sacrifices was the most important thing he could do to please God, but really obedience was. Sacrifice is essential when it is in obedience to God. But some are making sacrifices of prayer, fasting, and other spiritual activities in a performative way to earn righteousness or respect from other Christians, not in obedience to God. Some who read the Bible and pray daily are careless with their words and harbor jealousy and pride in their hearts. They think the most crucial part of relationship with God is checking off a list of spiritual activities like reading the Word and praying, so they neglect the aspects of life that seem less spiritual to them.

But the most important part of relationship with God is obedience—moment by moment, every day. When God is asking you to spend time with your kids and you are, at that moment you're obeying Him, and it's the most spiritual thing you can be doing. When God is asking you to clean the house and you obey Him in that, it's the most spiritual thing you can be doing in that moment.

To be a person after God's heart (Acts 13:22) means to be most passionate about doing His will and all that He is asking of you—and to follow through and carry out those things. God's whole heart is for His children to discover His love and receive His healing and deliverance.

His main way of reaching His people with His love and power is through His servants. Therefore, the work of God that takes place in God's anointed churches and ministries is the most important work in the world. Though God calls His believers to be vessels of Him in several aspects of society, the place where believers are equipped to be powerful vessels is the church. The church is also where the mightiest signs, wonders, and miracles take place because of the high-level anointing that is entrusted to the leaders of the church (Acts 2:43).

Obeying God by contributing to His work through serving, testifying, spreading the good news of what He is doing in the church, and sowing is such an important part of relationship with God. You are partnering with Him to do what He is most passionate about when you contribute to the work of God. That is intimacy! It is not just in prayer and reading the Word that intimacy with God is found. Intimacy will always be found when you're doing anything in obedience to God. Why? Because when you are obeying God, you are partnering with Him and touching His heart.

Chapter 12

MAINTAINING YOUR DELIVERANCE: BE PLANTED

O NE OF THE crucial principles in the kingdom of God, required of all believers, is to be planted in an anointed church where God is calling you.

> And he will be like a tree firmly planted [and fed] by streams of water, which yields its fruit in its season; its leaf does not wither; and in whatever he does, he prospers [and comes to maturity].
> —PSALM 1:3, AMP

The meaning of this scripture is clear: When you are planted at an anointed church, you will be fruitful in every season, you will prosper, and you will constantly overcome the enemy's schemes. This means that a huge key to walking in abundant life and continually having victory over the enemy is being and remaining planted.

An anointed church is one that is ordained by God, not man, and whose leader is anointed by God, not man. Being planted is one of the new-wine principles that many Christians do not know about or are unaware of the importance. Being planted means staying in one place, planted at one church.

> For even if you were to have ten thousand teachers [to guide you] in Christ, yet you would not have many fathers [who led you to Christ and assumed responsibility for you], for I became your father in Christ Jesus through the good news [of salvation]. So I urge you, be imitators of me [just as a child imitates his father]. For this reason I have sent Timothy to you, who is my beloved and faithful child in the Lord, and he will remind you of my way of life in Christ [my conduct and my precepts for godly living], just as I teach everywhere in every church.
>
> —1 Corinthians 4:15–17, AMP

This scripture speaks of the principle of being planted in one place, under one leader (spiritual mother or father). This principle is contrary to the "buffet culture" that most people follow today. Many television viewers use not just one streaming service but several. Most people use not just one social media platform but many. There are also a plethora of stores and restaurants to choose from.

Many think this buffet culture is the best kind of lifestyle. Yet in the spiritual realm the opposite is true. It's important that you don't drag your physical buffet culture lifestyle into your spiritual lifestyle. In the passage above, Paul told the Corinthians that they might have many teachers but he was their only spiritual parent. It's OK to watch other teachers from time to time, but your focus should be where you are planted; that is where your "spiritual GPS" is. It is where you will be guided in God's will, directed into your purpose, and equipped to fulfill your calling on this earth.

Each ministry has a vision. Where you are called to be planted relates to your purpose. What God is calling you to do is in line with what God is calling the ministry to—the ministry where He's led you to be planted.

For example, the church I pastor, 5F Church, has a vision to bring revival to the body of Christ and every nation. We are called to preach the full gospel, including the parts that need to be revived: that Jesus came to destroy the works of the devil here and now and that His power is available to deliver the oppressed and heal the sick.

We are called to be surrendered vessels whom God finds trustworthy to pour His anointing into. We are called to release His anointing to all who come to Him and to heal the sick, cast out demons, and raise the dead. We are called to release the new wine of sharing God's love and grace with people so they may be set free from spiritual blindness and the bondage of religion.

We are called to freely give what we have received, so the anointing must be imparted to others. We are called to make disciples of the nations, equipping leaders and all believers to be powerful vessels of God. God has called us to partner with Him to restore all that was lost in the Acts church: the anointing, fivefold ministry, apostles, prophets, purity and humility in the church, and God's principles and ways in His new wine, such as using unlikely "weak" and "foolish" vessels according to His choosing, not man's (1 Cor. 1:27).

You cannot fulfill your calling if you're not planted at the right place, because you must be equipped specifically for your calling—and the place where you are planted contains the spiritual GPS for your future. It is important that you are planted where God is calling you. I give 5F Church just as an example. Apply this example to your own life as you discern where God is leading you, whether it is 5F or another church. If your passions align with this vision, God may be calling you to be planted at 5F Church.

Be Planted for Equipping

> Now these are the gifts Christ gave to the church: the apostles, the prophets, the evangelists, and the pastors and teachers. Their responsibility is to equip God's people to do his work and build up the church, the body of Christ. This will continue until we all come to such unity in our faith and knowledge of God's Son that we will be mature in the Lord, measuring up to the full and complete standard of Christ.
>
> Then we will no longer be immature like children. We won't be tossed and blown about by every wind of new teaching. We will not be influenced when people try to trick us with lies so clever they sound like the truth. Instead, we will speak the truth in love, growing in every way more and more like Christ, who is the head of his body, the church. He makes the whole body fit together perfectly. As each part does its own special work, it helps the other parts grow, so that the whole body is healthy and growing and full of love.
>
> —Ephesians 4:11–16, nlt

"Their responsibility is to equip God's people" (v. 12). You *need* to be equipped, or else you will be spiritually blind and not prepared to defeat the enemy. Spiritual war is the most intense kind: "For we do not wrestle against flesh and blood, but against principalities, against powers, against the rulers of the darkness of this age, against spiritual hosts of wickedness in the heavenly places" (Eph. 6:12, NKJV).

Spiritual war involves battles against demonic powers and forces. Physical warriors train intensely in boot camp. How much more do you need to train for the spiritual battle you are in? You need spiritual training basically every day of your life! You need the prophetic anointing that moves through your leader(s) to reveal the sneaky schemes of the devil in real time.

I'm always amazed and humbled to hear testimonies of those who are planted at my church sharing that they *needed* the word that was preached that week. People constantly testify of how they were able to have victory over the enemy because of the equipping they received that week. The equipping you will receive in the place you are planted is sent by God to save you from the enemy's attacks. It's sent to open your spiritual eyes so the devil can't outwit you and trap you with his sneaky schemes. "Now the serpent was more crafty (subtle, skilled in deceit) than any living creature of the field which the LORD God had made" (Gen. 3:1, AMP). So much of your victory over the devil will result from the spiritual muscles and insight you receive through the teachings found at the place where you are planted.

"Their responsibility is to equip God's people to do his work" (Eph. 4:12, NLT). The fivefold ministers also equip you to do God's work, to be a powerful vessel for Him and fulfill your purpose. Part of this equipping includes impartation. Impartation of anointing comes when you are planted under *one* spiritual mother or father, such as Elisha was planted under Elijah, Joshua under Moses, and Timothy under Paul. To be fully equipped to fulfill your purpose, you need revelation and knowledge as well as the power of God.

PROTECTION

> Have confidence in your leaders and submit to their authority, because they keep watch over you as those who must give an account. Do this so that their work will be a joy, not a burden, for that would be of no benefit to you.
>
> —HEBREWS 13:17

Did you know that your spiritual parent keeps watch over you? God entrusts them to watch over your spiritual health and protection. You see, much of what God does for you He does through a vessel. Take me for an example. So much of the spiritual growth I've received has been through God moving through my spiritual father. So much of the direction and guidance I've received from God has come through my spiritual father. The way I found my calling was from God speaking through a prophet, my spiritual father. The majority of the correction I've received has come by God moving through my spiritual father.

At the church where you are planted, you receive not just teaching and equipping but also protection. When it comes to maintaining your deliverance, being protected is *vital*. The main way God protects you is *through* your spiritual leader and the church where you are planted.

This protection comes in two ways. First, being planted is a spiritual principle. When you obey a spiritual principle, supernatural benefits are unlocked. Supernatural protection is unlocked the moment you make the covenant to be planted where God is calling you. Make this covenant by simply responding to what God is asking of you. You can speak aloud, "I plant myself here at this ministry _____. _____ is my spiritual mother/father. I will remain planted here with humility and loyalty in accordance with what God has directed me."

The anointing that flows from your spiritual leader is not just for casting out demons. It is also to protect you. The anointing flowing from your leader comes on your life as a constant spiritual protection. When demons see the anointing that covers you and protects you, they flee! No one—not even witches or warlocks—can put curses on you when you're planted (as long as you keep doors shut and reject bad words from people). But when you don't follow this spiritual principle, you are not accessing this supernatural protection. Some people have curses and oppression in their lives simply because they are not planted. They are not accessing the fullness of protection that God intends for them.

Second, protection comes through your spiritual leader's teaching and prophetic words, as well as their correction and guidance. God knows the devil's schemes. He will direct your leader to bring prophetic warning, proper guidance, and equipping for you to have victory over these schemes, ultimately guiding you to safety.

If you are not sure where to be planted yet or if you're currently in a church without God's power, you do not need worry that you are left unprotected. God's grace is covering you. However, once you're aware of this important truth, it's essential to take action. God's grace goes where He's calling you. You need to be obedient to stay in His grace. God wants all His children to be planted in one place and not drifting constantly from church to church. He will be faithful to lead you where He wants you planted, as long as you're humble and open to hearing His voice guiding you.

> Remain in Me, and I [will remain] in you. Just as no branch can bear fruit by itself without remaining in the vine, neither can you [bear fruit, producing evidence of your faith] unless you remain in Me. I am the Vine; you are the branches. The one who remains in Me and I in him bears much fruit, for [otherwise] apart from Me [that is, cut off from vital union with Me] you can do nothing. If anyone does not remain in Me, he is thrown out like a [broken off] branch, and withers and dies; and they gather such branches and throw them into the fire, and they are burned. If you remain in Me and My words remain in you [that is, if we are vitally united and My message lives in your heart], ask whatever you wish and it will be done for you. My Father is glorified and honored by this, when you bear much fruit, and prove yourselves to be My [true] disciples.
> —John 15:4–8, amp

To remain in God, you need to honor and follow His ways of bringing protection, equipping, and impartation. You must remain planted and follow the principles of being planted to stay safe and bear good fruit. If you do not remain in God by following His ways, spiritual danger and harm may come.

How to Know Where You're Supposed to Be Planted

Once you fully surrender to the Holy Spirit's leading, He will guide you where He wants you to be planted. You must surrender traditions, a desire to be liked or understood, the desire to be free of persecution, and "inside the box" ways, because where God is calling you to be planted will be where His power is. And wherever God's power is, there will also be persecution.

Ministries that carry His power attract the most persecution because the devil is most terrified of ministries that actually destroy his kingdom. God also uses weak and foolish vessels who tend to be unlikely choices. This can mean they are young instead of traditionally older. This can mean they are female instead of traditionally male. Perhaps they have not attended a traditional Bible school but instead have been equipped and trained by their anointed spiritual parent. Perhaps they're not popular, they don't have the traditional appearance of a pastor, and they're not the most eloquent of speakers.

You need to surrender to the "outside the box" ways of God. Once you do that, only then will you be able to hear His voice guiding you to be planted at a specific ministry. God will speak to you through wisdom by helping you apply His Word to discern which ministry is from Him.

> You will know them by their fruits. Do men gather grapes from thornbushes or figs from thistles? Even so, every good tree bears good fruit, but a bad tree bears bad fruit. A good tree cannot bear bad fruit, nor can a bad tree bear good fruit. Every tree that does not bear good fruit is cut down and thrown into the fire. Therefore by their fruits you will know them.
> —Matthew 7:16–20, nkjv

You will know which ministry God is calling you to by applying this scripture. You will know a church is anointed and the leader truly sent by God if they produce fruit. The "fruit" relates to two parts: character and ministry.

In terms of character, does the leader have the fruits of the Holy Spirit (Gal. 5:22–23) in their words *and* actions? Is the leader truly humble? When persecution comes and people speak against them, do they still act in humility, or do they try to prove themselves? Do they seem quite offended and angry that people may view them incorrectly? Does the leader truly love? That can be tested by how they treat their enemies, for even unbelievers love those who are kind to them (Matt. 5:46–47). Is the leader selfless, giving the glory to God, or do they point to themself?

As far as fruits of the ministry, is the leader truly doing what Jesus commissioned? Jesus instructed the disciples, "As you go, preach, saying, 'The kingdom of heaven is at hand.' Heal the sick, cleanse the lepers, raise the dead, cast out demons. Freely you have received, freely give" (Matt. 10:7–8, NKJV).

Does the leader preach that the kingdom of heaven is at hand? This includes telling people not only that Jesus paid the price to save them from hell when they die but also that they can be freed from the devil's grip *now*. It means telling people that God's power is available to heal and deliver them now. It means being unafraid and unashamed to talk about the reality of demons and teach that Jesus can free people of any demonic power. It means teaching about God's kingdom, which includes the foundation of the apostles and prophets with Christ Jesus as the chief cornerstone (Eph. 2:20). It means explaining that you'll know for sure the kingdom of God has come when you experience or witness demons being cast out.

Jesus said, "If I drive out demons by the finger of God, then the kingdom of God has come upon you" (Luke 11:20).

Are the sick being healed and the oppressed set free? You'll discern whether these fruits are evident through people's testimonies, not through manifestations. When there are many testimonies, you'll know the manifestations are indeed the power of God making demons tremble and touching people so powerfully there are physical reactions to what is happening in the spirit.

Are people being saved and truly surrendering? Or is the emphasis more on the number of hands raised after an altar call? Are people's lives actually being transformed because they have encountered the power of God? Are people becoming more like Jesus? When you listen to the teachings from the ministry, are you spiritually transformed? Have you seen change in your life and yokes destroyed off your life if that was needed? Has the ministry helped you grow closer to God and opened your spiritual eyes? Have you been equipped for spiritual victory over the enemy? If so, you're experiencing true fruits! It is the anointing that reveals God's love, brings transformation, opens spiritual eyes, and equips one for victory. That's how you'll know whether there is good fruit or not.

Of the ministries that are anointed and have good fruit, how do you know which one you're supposed to be planted at exactly? The Holy Spirit will speak to your spirit and give you confirmations. If the ministry's vision and mission excite you and you feel passionate about the mission, it's a sign that this is where you're supposed to be planted. Also, you may feel an unexplainable connection and peace with a certain anointed ministry—a "knowing" that this is where God is calling you to be planted.

When spiritual warfare tries to pull you away from being planted there, that should be a confirmation rather than a discouragement. The devil knows the power of being planted exactly where God is calling you. The devil knows you will cause the most destruction to his kingdom when you are planted in the church where God has destined you to be.

Please understand that the church where God is calling you to be planted does not have to be in the city or nation where you live. Being planted is a spiritual principle, not a physical one. You can receive equipping, impartation, and spiritual protection through listening and receiving online just as well as in person. That being said, it is extremely important to travel and go to events or services in person as God leads and as often as possible when provision allows.

As I write this, we are only in the beginning stages of this end-time revival. At this stage the anointing, the new wine, and anointed churches are rare. Therefore, God *absolutely* is calling many people to be planted in an anointed church that is not in their city or nation, because it's important to be planted in the right church. The "best" church in your city is not good enough. It must be a truly anointed church and the right church for you.

People planted at 5F Church come from more than 150 nations (many planted virtually who tune in online)! Thousands across many different countries have testified that they have been equipped, healed, and delivered through this ministry. They have grown spiritually, received impartation, and been brought closer to Jesus. They were protected and are now walking in victory over the enemy. The people who are planted from afar have been blessed and touched by God just as much as those who live in Los Angeles, where 5F Church is located.

Every week people testify of all kinds of miracles and encounters with God that they have experienced *through the screen* as they watch live streams, replays, and other 5F Church videos online. All glory to God! I share this testimony about 5F Church to give you an example of one of the places around the world where God is moving in limitless power. It's important to know just how powerfully God is moving so you do not limit yourself and stay in a place where you're not being spiritually fed and healed.

HOW TO BE PLANTED

Being planted is not simply attending only one church week after week. It includes being a true disciple. "Then Jesus said to his disciples, 'If any of you wants to be my follower, you must give up your own way, take up your cross, and follow me'" (Matt. 16:24, NLT). *You must give up your own way!* You must give up your old wine, your old religious ways. You must humble yourself and be like a teachable child so God can pour the new wine into you and teach you new things.

This applies to all, including those who have been believers for many years or have even been ministers. You need to lay down your vision and accept the vision of the ministry you are planted at. Humble yourself, and be ready to throw out wrong doctrine that you thought was right. Be open and ready for correction. Give up your own way of being a Christian and of doing ministry, and instead follow the ways being taught where you are planted. Value the teachings, and treat them as the precious treasure and life source they are. If it is at all possible, do not miss a Sunday and/or midweek service or live stream. Meditate on the Word, take notes, listen again, and intentionally apply the Word in your life.

Another aspect of "being planted" is serving God specifically at the ministry where you're planted. It's important to contribute to the work of God, not just be on the receiving end. This is also a crucial part of receiving impartation, as exemplified by Elisha, who served his spiritual father, Elijah (1 Kings 19:21). If you live in the city where your church is, there are more opportunities to serve. If, however, you live in a different city, one way to serve among others is to do your best to share what God is doing at the church. Use your social media for God's glory, and share posts, videos, testimonies, miracles, sermons, and preaching moments. Share your own testimony as well. Share with your family, friends, coworkers, and others you encounter.

The last part of being planted involves tithing and sowing.

> "Bring the whole tithe into the storehouse, that there may be food in my house. Test me in this," says the LORD Almighty, "and see if I will not throw open the floodgates of heaven and pour out so much blessing that there will not be room enough to store it."
> —MALACHI 3:10

The word *storehouse* today refers to the church where you are planted. You have a responsibility to do your part in bringing the tithe (10 percent of your income) to where you're fed spiritually. When everyone does their part, there will be enough provision for the work of God to continue and go forth with excellence. It's also important to be a generous and cheerful giver, giving beyond 10 percent when you're able.

If you are missing any of these aspects of being planted in a church, you're not fully rooted. Make being planted in a church where God is moving in power a priority—and watch what happens!

Chapter 13

MAINTAINING YOUR DELIVERANCE: VALUE IT

WHAT YOU VALUE you will protect. The more you value something, the greater the lengths you will go to protect it. When something costs a lot of money, you will pay a great amount to put insurance on it. The more valuable items you have in your house, the greater measures you will take to install security. If you carry a valuable item around with you, do you notice how much more conscientious you are to guarantee it isn't lost compared to other items?

When it comes to maintaining your deliverance and whatever blessing God has given you, you *must* value what you received or you will lose it. In this chapter you'll learn exactly how to "add the insurance" and "set up the security system" on your freedom and all that God has blessed you with.

In the previous chapter you learned the connection between maintaining your deliverance and being planted. You must protect this precious gift of your covering and source of spiritual food and guidance. The devil knows the power of being planted, so he will try to get you to uproot yourself. One of his schemes in doing this is to work through other people in the church to hurt, offend, or annoy you. To overcome this scheme, you need to understand that there is not a single church where all the church members are perfect.

It's vital that you are able to trust the leadership at the church where God has called you to be planted, because that is a major way God will speak to you, guide you, and protect you (Heb. 13:17). But you certainly cannot expect that all or most believers in the church are spiritually mature.

Everyone is at a different stage in their journey. Some are babies in Christ who have freshly come from life in the world. Some are lukewarm. And others, though the minority, are wolves (Matt. 7:15). Every church has some who attend and participate with wrong intentions. And some are either knowingly or unknowingly being used by the enemy to try to pull people away from the church where God ordained them to be planted.

If you experience hurt from someone at church, or if something has offended you, it's very important to renew your mind with the truth of what's really going on spiritually and recognize that this spiritual attack is designed to pull you away from where you are planted.

Renew your mind with the truth that the person who hurt you does not represent the leadership of the church. Do not be fooled by this trap of the enemy. "A person's wisdom yields patience; it is to one's glory to overlook an offense" (Prov. 19:11).

God never wants you to be offended. You're obeying God if you reject the temptation of offense. We are called to be servants and to "regard others as more important" than ourselves (Phil. 2:3, AMP). That means we should not feel entitled to respect. To keep offense in your heart is to be self-absorbed, and that is exactly what the devil wants. If you find yourself having thoughts of offense toward another person, reject those thoughts so you may then bless and pray for that person. If hurt from church members is causing you to fear or have less motivation to attend church, renew your mind with the truth that this is the devil's scheme to pull you away. Forgive the person, and open your heart to God as He brings total healing to you so your peace and joy can be restored.

"For where your treasure is, there your heart will be also" (Matt. 6:21). If you don't make the determination, you will take your blessings for granted. Make a practice of regularly reflecting on the blessings God has sent you and thanking Him for them. You might have received powerful deliverance, healing, and transformation at the church where you're planted. You might have received significant blessings over time. But years have passed, and it's easy to forget what life was like before you attended this particular church. If this extraordinary and unusual life has become normal and ordinary for you, intentionally renew your mind and remember what life was like before. Renew your mind by remembering that your life is so blessed because of Jesus—and especially Him moving through the church where you're planted.

The devil is described as "the accuser of our brethren" (Rev. 12:10, NKJV). One of his great schemes is to try to get people to leave their churches by bringing false accusations against servants of God and their ministries. When you hear accusations about your leader and ministry, it's very important to remember that the devil *will* falsely accuse true servants of God and their ministries. Therefore, you must not be quick to believe everything you hear.

Many people who falsely "expose" ministers clearly have bad fruit. By the way they speak, you can tell they are judgmental, religious (stuck in old wine), prideful, jealous, and hateful. If a person exhibits these qualities, they are disqualified to give you spiritual direction. Even if one doesn't appear to have bad fruit, consider who the person is. Is God calling you to listen to them for spiritual direction? In most cases the answer is no. Be aware of this scheme of the enemy, and walk in wisdom to make sure you don't fall for the trap of the devil, who is trying to pull you out of the church by his false accusations.

It's essential to value the true anointing that is flowing on your life. When you are positioned under the anointing and a servant of God declares a word over your life, such as "Be healed" or "This spirit must go," value that anointed word! The Roman centurion valued Jesus and the word He declared when he was seeking healing for his servant. He knew that when Jesus just spoke a word, his servant would be healed! The centurion's faith released the miracle (Matt. 8:5–13). Isaiah 55:11 says, "So shall My word be that goes forth from My mouth; it shall not return to Me void, but it shall accomplish what I please, and it shall prosper in the thing for which I sent it" (NKJV).

When an anointed servant of God speaks, the word must come to pass! Many people are losing their miracles before the miracles manifest from the spiritual realm to the physical realm. A servant of God speaks a word such as "Cancer must go" or "This spirit must go," and the person on the receiving end disvalues the word completely. They act like the words carry no power. They start demanding one-on-one prayer. After the service ends, they ask many people to pray for them. They leave the church thinking that nothing happened.

This is such a shame because the miracle was released through the word, but they missed it! When a person throws you a ball, you have to lift your arms and open your hands to catch it. If you leave your arms at your sides, the ball will pass over your head or bounce away. You had an easy opportunity to catch the ball, but you chose to completely miss it. It is the same way with receiving miracles in the presence of an anointed servant of God. The servant of God is "throwing" miracles at you with their words, but you must lift your hands and "catch" the miracles to receive them!

The action of "catching your miracle" is believing and choosing to value the words declared. So many testimonies of miracles are taking place in the ministries of true anointed servants of God. For example, in my ministry many individuals have testified that they received their miracles just by watching online from across the world and without me praying for them one-on-one! So, if you hear all those testimonies, what excuse do you have to not "catch" the miracle? What excuse do you have to not value the words declared? If you need help to believe in this area, I encourage you to go to my YouTube channel and watch the Testimonies playlist (@ApostleKathrynKrick).

When the words are spoken by an anointed servant, miracles immediately come on you in the spiritual realm. For some, the miracles will manifest into the physical realm right away. For others, this may take some time.

> Now on his way to Jerusalem, Jesus traveled along the border between Samaria and Galilee. As he was going into a village, ten men who had leprosy met him. They stood at a distance and called out in a loud voice, "Jesus, Master, have pity on us!"
>
> When he saw them, he said, "Go, show

yourselves to the priests." And as they went, they were cleansed.

—LUKE 17:11–14

Once you've received the word declared, immediately be intentional about taking steps to maintain your miracle. You need to protect the miracle that is currently unseen to make sure it does not get aborted before it has a chance to manifest in the physical realm. You protect it by receiving the miracle in your heart by faith and speaking aloud "I receive my healing" or "I receive that word" or "I believe I am healed!"

Also, immediately thank God. You can pray something like this:

> *Thank You, Jesus, for delivering me! I believe it has just happened in the spiritual realm when Your servant declared the word. I believe I will see it manifest in the physical realm soon. Thank You for Your anointing that has just healed me!*

Continue to declare that you're healed, and continue to thank Jesus until you see the miracle manifest fully. Once the miracle has manifested fully, keep thanking God for this blessing.

When you do not see the miracle manifest immediately, the enemy may try to attack your mind with thoughts of doubt like these: "Nothing happened"; "You don't have enough faith"; "Your case is hopeless"; "You didn't feel anything, so nothing must've happened" (especially when others are feeling things, falling back, and/or weeping); or "You must need one-on-one prayer." If you get these thoughts, renew your mind, reminding yourself that this is the devil lying to you, trying to steal the miracle that Jesus has just done. You must go into warrior mode and fiercely protect this precious miracle you've received from Jesus.

The way you protect the miracle against this attack is by submitting to God's truth, resisting the devil, and rejecting the devil's lies with your words (Jas. 4:7). Declare something like this: "I reject these lies that I'm not set free and healed. I have just been set free/healed, and I will soon see the miracle manifest fully. I value this miracle that God just released to me. Thank You, Jesus, for healing me!" It's possible that the devil will bring these lies repeatedly. You must be vigilant and keep on rejecting him, declaring the truth, and thanking God. As you keep resisting the devil and submitting to God's truth, the devil will flee and you will see victory! You will see the miracle manifest!

THE BIGGEST SCHEME TO STEAL YOUR FREEDOM

The enemy's most prevalent scheme to steal your freedom is to get you to think that demons have come back or to convince you that no deliverance actually occurred. Once you're set free from demonic oppression, demons that were inside (your soul or body) are no longer there. You are no longer oppressed by demonic chains. However, you are not set free from a spiritual war. The devil does not completely disappear. None of us are free from living in a spiritual war until we go to heaven. But now that you are free, you can run your race without heavy chains shackled to your ankles. Now you have nothing hindering you from constant victory.

> In all these things we are more than conquerors and
> gain an overwhelming victory through Him who
> loved us [so much that He died for us].
>
> —ROMANS 8:37, AMP

Honestly, before you were set free, you did not have an "overwhelming victory" because the devil held an area of victory in your life. But now that you're free, Jesus has made you a constant champion who conquers battle after battle and gains that overwhelming victory! This is a part of your inheritance as a child of God and a promise from God. As long as you obey Him and have faith with works (faith in action; see James 2:14), you will have overwhelming victory, because "greater is he that is in you [Jesus], than he that is in the world [the devil]" (1 John 4:4, KJV).

The devil may bring attacks in the form of lies, saying that you're not free or that demons have returned. These lies may feel just like the attacks he brought when you were oppressed in the past. But they are actually different. These are external spiritual attacks, not internal demons. They are weapons formed against you, and you can stop them from prospering simply by submitting to God's truth as you renew your mind and resist the devil's lies.

> Dear friends, do not be surprised at the fiery ordeal
> that has come on you to test you, as though some-
> thing strange were happening to you.
>
> —1 PETER 4:12

God allows the devil to attack you at times for a purpose! There's always a purpose, and it's for your good. "You intended to harm me, but God intended it for good to accomplish what is now being done, the saving of many lives" (Gen. 50:20). God will allow attacks from the enemy when He knows He can use them as a refining fire that will stretch your faith and mold your character to be godlier. God wants to use you to save lost, oppressed, and sick souls on this earth. That can happen only if He takes you through the refining fire to make you into a pure vessel who can properly steward the anointing He wants to release to you.

If the enemy is bringing attacks by lying to you about your deliverance, know that God is testing your faith. He wants your faith to be stretched. "Without faith it is impossible to please God" (Heb. 11:6). You can please God only if you have faith, and the more faith you have, the more God can do through you—which is what's most pleasing to Him.

The attacks the devil may bring outwardly can mimic the former demonic oppression you had, but you must realize it's all a lie, a facade. If you will stand firm in your faith and reject the devil's lies, *he must flee*! The attacks must stop!

Here are some examples of the ways the devil can mimic demonic oppression. You may have suffered from mental torment in the past, such as suicidal thoughts or other demonic voices. No matter how many times you rejected the lies, they would not stop until you received deliverance. Once you're set free and after some time passes, the devil may speak these same lies outwardly, and they can feel exactly the same as when you had demonic oppression. But this time, as you reject the voices, they must cease. In some cases the voices may not immediately stop, but you must keep rejecting them. Eventually they must go.

If you were healed of a disease, the devil can try to mimic the sickness to make you think you're sick again.

You may experience pain or symptoms. You must know that this is a spiritual weapon that you do not have to let prosper and turn into actual sickness again! The devil can come in all sorts of sneaky ways. My spiritual father told me a story of how a man came to his church and was healed from a disease, and then he went to get an X-ray. The X-ray showed something seriously wrong, as if the disease was still there or something worse. The man had another X-ray taken at a different hospital, and this time the X-ray showed no disease! Come to find out, the first X-ray had some object blocking the camera that made it look as if something was in his body.

The devil can use all kinds of tricks to try to deceive you into thinking the sickness or oppression has returned. You must be aware of these schemes and remember the reality of your miracle. Also remember that because you are a child of God, the devil is *not allowed* to steal what God has given you! "Therefore, my dear brothers and sisters, stand firm. Let nothing move you" (1 Cor. 15:58). And finally, "fight the good fight of the faith [in the conflict with evil]" (1 Tim. 6:12, AMP).

It's so important that you reject these lies of the devil. Otherwise, if you speak words such as "I guess I didn't really get healed" or "I guess the demons came back," you are opening the door for the enemy to bring the sickness or oppression back. It's the opposite of resisting the weapon that is formed against you. By speaking words like this, you may be allowing the weapon to prosper.

MIMICKING DEMONIC MANIFESTATIONS

As he thinks in his heart, so is he.

—PROVERBS 23:7, NKJV

The mind is so powerful. What you choose to meditate on and believe will become your reality. You will act as you think. If you constantly think "I am not smart," you will never challenge yourself or try anything difficult. If you have this mindset, you will never know your potential, and you'll live at a lower level of intellect, accepting a career and life of mediocrity, perhaps even poverty. This would all be a result of what you chose to believe and meditate on. On the contrary, if you constantly meditate on God's words and promises, you will see all His promises come to pass.

The devil entices some into thinking they need more deliverance when they're already free. God delivers some people layer by layer. The more complex the oppression, oftentimes the longer the process takes to be completely free. However, when a person is planted where high-level anointing is released and they are surrendered and using all the keys to receive complete deliverance, they should not need additional heavy deliverance after months or a year of being a serious, planted disciple.

If a person has gone through layers of deliverance and is fully free, the devil wants them to keep seeking deliverance, thinking they're still entrapped. It's like the analogy of an animal tied to a pole and then the owner cuts the rope. The animal is free to leave the spot they were trapped in for so long. But because they're not aware that they're free and able to leave, they stay in that same place. This is what the enemy tries to do in some people's lives. He doesn't want them to move forward and fulfill their purposes. He doesn't want them to go from glory to glory and walk in abundance, because that gives glory to God and shames the devil.

Some people are enslaved by their own thoughts that are

influenced by the devil. They can actually fake a manifestation because the mind is so powerful. For instance, if the devil convinces a freed person that they still have demons and brings a thought (outwardly) such as "The demon is trying to come out of your throat now," the person may start coughing. Or if the devil sends another thought suggesting, "The demon is coming out with a scream now," the person may start screaming. But it's completely in the mind. Their mind made their body do drastic things.

I've seen this scheme of the enemy as I've ministered. God revealed to me prophetically what was going on, and He led me to tell the person (who was fake manifesting) what was happening in the spiritual realm. Each time I shared with the person that they were indeed free and that the devil was just lying to them, the fake manifestations stopped. The person did not fake manifest again and was finally able to move forward. This enabled the person to now walk in abundant life and be a powerful tool in God's hands, contributing to His work instead of being stuck in the same place.

> If you abide in my word, you are truly my disciples, and you will know the truth, and the truth will set you free.
>
> —JOHN 8:31–32, ESV

If the devil is bringing fake manifestations and thoughts of oppression from the past, you will get victory by putting into practice what I shared in chapter 11: Fill yourself daily by reading God's Word and pursuing a relationship with Jesus. Keep declaring "I am free! Thank You, Jesus, for freeing me." Keep rejecting the devil's lies.

How will you know whether you are fully free or need

more deliverance? Carefully apply and value all the keys used to unlock and receive complete deliverance that are presented in this book. Be a true disciple of what I have taught in this book. Apply all I have taught, and just rest.

Do not become obsessed with seeking deliverance, such as desiring to manifest so you can have one-on-one prayer. This type of obsession, versus seeking Jesus and resting in His timing, can be an open door for the devil to fool you into thinking you still have more demons. As long as you just rest in Jesus, rely on His perfect timing in bringing about the full manifestation of the miracles, and keep being obedient to the principles I've shared in this book, you *will* be fully free.

TESTIFY

> They overcame him by the blood of the Lamb, and by the word of their testimony.
> —REVELATION 12:11, KJV

When you testify, you overcome the devil! This is a spiritual principle. It is one of the supernatural keys of overcoming the devil's attacks to steal your miracle, and it has to do with the power of your words. As you testify, you solidify what happened in the spiritual realm. It's an action of receiving the miracle and saying, "This is mine, and I am keeping it."

Also, all the benefits from Jesus come *when* you surrender to Him, obey Him, and give Him glory. If you are not doing one or all of these things, you are opening a door to the enemy. When God performs a miracle for you, it's so important that you give Him the full glory by thanking Him personally and sharing your testimony.

"The testimony of Jesus is the spirit of prophecy"

(Rev. 19:10, NKJV). When you testify about what Jesus has done in your life, you're releasing a "spirit of prophecy" that comes on whoever is listening, and this supernaturally lifts their faith. As you testify, you're prophesying the same miracle and other miracles to happen to whoever is listening. Your testimony is so powerful! God wants to do so many miracles through it.

Do you value Jesus? Do you value what He did for you? Do you want to please Jesus by testifying so others can receive, which in turn glorifies Him? If the answer is yes, do not hold back your testimony! Do you value the anointing that destroyed the yoke in your life? Then testify! There is so much skepticism and persecution toward anointed servants of God, and so many people are staying bound and sick because of this. Your testimony is *needed* to open eyes so people can see that the anointing from Jesus is real—and so they may be set free and healed!

You should not feel pressured to testify publicly of every single miracle God does for you each day, but make sure to testify when He delivers you, heals you, or does other major miracles. Do not be ashamed of how and where you received your miracle. The vessel God used to heal or deliver you may be controversial and may be a target of hate from others. Anyone who is anointed will indeed be controversial and hated, just as Jesus was (John 15:18–25).

Be brave and unashamed of God and all His ways. Be unashamed of how He uses anointed vessels, especially those who are considered "weak" and "foolish." Be unashamed of the anointing that delivers you yet also makes the religious uncomfortable. Be unashamed that you were in need of a deliverer and Jesus saved and freed you. Do not water down your testimony to try to make it more comfortable for others. Share where you received your miracle and how it happened so others can know how and where to encounter the power of God just as you have. The Bible says to give honor where honor is due (Rom. 13:7). It's important to give servants of God honor and to testify of the fruit exhibited in their ministry so God's work can go forth more and more through that ministry.

Sow a Gratitude Seed

Once you have been delivered, it's wise to give thanks to God through sacrifice. Being delivered is a huge work that God has done. It's essential to show Him the proper gratitude—not just in word but also in action. Deliverance and healing are free gifts from God. Yet we must not see them as cheap. Sowing is an action step that will lead you to valuing your deliverance more, as you're putting a treasure (money) into thanking God.

Everything you sow is truly a seed, and it will produce fruit. There is a reaping with every seed, even if you are sowing to God simply out of obedience or gratitude. When you sow a seed thanking God for your deliverance, you can expect a reaping of more anointing, specifically in the area of helping you maintain your deliverance. If you are planted where the anointing is, you are covered and protected. But at times, it is wise to sow into the anointing to reap greater anointing for added protection, especially if the enemy has brought an attack. As you sow, more anointing will come on you to strengthen you spiritually so you can have victory over every scheme of the enemy in his attempt to return.

THE POWER OF PATIENCE

The last piece of wisdom I'll share on maintaining your deliverance is that you should be patient and humble in your deliverance journey.

You must consistently do your part of applying the spiritual principles I've outlined. Be a good soldier as you fight the good fight of faith. If the battle feels intense at first, know that it is because the enemy is mad, but also remember that he is a loser! The difficult part of your journey will not last forever. Maybe you're still close to the shores of "Egypt," but with each day you're moving farther and farther away. With each day of victory over the enemy, you grow in the spiritual realm.

Remember that every time you reject the devil's lies, God sees, and He's so proud of you. He's with you, helping you, strengthening you, and cheering you on. Always renew your mind to see God's love for you. His love is your source of strength in the battle. Leaning on His love by seeing His love accurately allows you access to His power, the mighty power that brings victory.

God's timing of bringing the manifestation of total deliverance and healing is different for everyone. Sometimes it may seem like you're delayed in reaching the promised land, but this is because God is more interested in the transformation of your heart than a quick fix. Trust Him. Just keep doing what He's instructed you to do through this book and you will absolutely see increased breakthroughs every day until you find all the bondage is completely gone!

So if the Son sets you free, you will be free indeed.
—JOHN 8:36

Let me speak the following over you:

I declare that no demon can come back to you. I release this anointing, and I speak protection over you. I declare that your mind will be sound and peaceful. May you increase in wisdom now and every day. May you have victory after victory over the devil every single day. May the devil never fool you. May you see spiritually and discern every scheme and attack of the devil. May you conquer every battle, and may you have overwhelming victory.

Chapter 14

COMMON DELIVERANCE MISCONCEPTIONS

NOW THAT YOU'VE received deliverance and learned how to maintain your freedom, I'm going to share some more insight into the spiritual realm so you will be fully equipped to live a life of victory and walk in godly confidence. In this last chapter I'll be addressing some common questions you may have about deliverance and the misconceptions concerning it.

IF I NEED DELIVERANCE, SHOULD I FAST?

Many fast food as a way to receive something from God or to become more spiritual. It's true that fasting can help you deny your flesh and strengthen your spirit, but this happens only when the fast is Spirit-led. Do not practice the old-wine, religious way of fasting that is based on tradition. Nor should you fast in a manipulative way, bargaining with God so He will give you something in return.

The main purpose of fasting is to deny your flesh in areas of strong temptation so your body may be subdued and your spirit can rise higher. God will call you to fast—to deny your flesh—primarily in the area where your flesh is strong. Many people fast food even though their strong temptations are not to overeat but to be on social media for many hours. In this case the wise way to fast would be to deny themselves social media for a time.

The amount of time for fasting should be Spirit-led. It does not have to be forty days or something drastic. Sometimes it can be just half a day. (If you're fasting social media, make sure not to fast your spiritual food: the live stream or replay of church. Once the service is finished, you can immediately get off the social media platform.)

> Then John's disciples came and asked him, "How is it that we and the Pharisees fast often, but your disciples do not fast?"
>
> Jesus answered, "How can the guests of the bridegroom mourn while he is with them? The time will come when the bridegroom will be taken from them; then they will fast.
>
> "No one sews a patch of unshrunk cloth on an old garment, for the patch will pull away from the garment, making the tear worse. Neither do people pour new wine into old wineskins. If they do, the skins will burst; the wine will run out and the wineskins will be ruined. No, they pour new wine into new wineskins, and both are preserved."
>
> —MATTHEW 9:14–17

The Pharisees and John the Baptist's disciples were fasting in the old-wine, religious way. Jesus did not require His disciples to fast while He was with them because it was time for the disciples to be busy with the work of God. God did not have a purpose for them to fast at that point. Rather, He was leading them to focus on other ways to deny the flesh and grow spiritually during this specific season.

In this passage Jesus is sharing a new revelation of how to fast, led by the Spirit rather than by religion and tradition. To receive and understand this new revelation, individuals needed to humble themselves and shed their old wineskins—their old doctrines and ways of interpreting the Word.

There can be times when God leads you to fast food even if you don't have temptations to be gluttonous. The act of denying your flesh does make your spirit arise and your flesh decrease when your fasting is led by the Spirit. For example, Jesus fasted for forty days when the Holy Spirit led Him to be tempted in the wilderness.

If a person has severe demonic oppression from giving the devil many footholds, it is wise to fast before attending a service (in person or online) where the anointing will be released, as fasting weakens the demons' grip. Still, this type of fasting should always be Spirit-led. This direction to fast before going to receive deliverance is not an instruction for all believers. But if you feel the Spirit's leading and/or you know you have deep oppression, definitely fast before positioning yourself under the anointing.

DOES A MINISTER NEED TO FAST AND PRAY TO CAST OUT STRONG DEMONS?

When they approached the crowd, a man came up to Jesus, kneeling before Him and saying, "Lord, have mercy on my son, for he is a lunatic (moonstruck) and suffers terribly; for he often falls into the fire and often into the water. And I brought him to Your disciples, and they were not able to heal him." And Jesus answered, "You unbelieving and perverted generation, how long shall I be with you? How long shall I put up with you? Bring him here to Me." Jesus rebuked the demon, and it came out of him, and the boy was healed at once.

Then the disciples came to Jesus privately and asked, "Why could we not drive it out?" He answered, "Because of your little faith [your lack of trust and confidence in the power of God]; for I assure you and most solemnly say to you, if you have [living] faith the size of a mustard seed, you will say to this mountain, 'Move from here to there,' and [if it is God's will] it will move; and nothing will be impossible for you. [But this kind of demon does not go out except by prayer and fasting.]"

—Matthew 17:14–21, amp

In this story Jesus did not tell the parent to bring the boy back after He'd taken time to fast and pray so He could cast out the demon. Yet many people think that's what this scripture is saying, as if a ritual needs to be performed before some demons can be cast out.

When Jesus refers to "prayer and fasting" here, He is not suggesting that if you pray for so many hours straight, you will receive more anointing to cast out demons. Remember what I taught on prayer in chapter 11. God sees you as genuinely drawing close to Him and engaging in true prayer and intimacy as you include Him throughout your day. You are in true relationship with Him when you nurture a healthy fear of God by holding Him in high respect and continually obeying Him as a way of touching His heart. When this kind of true prayer and intimacy are present, God sees that He can entrust you with more anointing, and He then pours out higher levels of anointing to deal with higher-level demonic cases. (This also depends on your calling, as not all are called to cast out high-level demons.)

As I noted above, the main purpose of fasting is to deny your flesh in the area where it is strong. So, if you're not denying your flesh where it is strong, you are being carnal and not spiritually mature. In this case God will not pour out more anointing until you're surrendered and taking your spiritual walk seriously.

Really what Jesus meant by saying "This kind of demon does not go out except by prayer and fasting," then, is that the disciples needed to be less carnal and more serious about their surrender, obedience, and daily walk with God. Then God could entrust them with more anointing.

DOES A MINISTER NEED TO SPEAK SPECIFIC WORDS WHEN CASTING OUT DEMONS?

It doesn't matter what specific words are used to cast out demons. What matters is that a servant of God is truly anointed and carries authority over the demon. It is crucial that the servant of God executes their authority properly, in the new-wine way versus the old-wine religious and traditional way.

When students are being loud, a teacher can say, "Be quiet" or "Stop being loud" or "Cut it out" or "That's enough" or "On the count of three, there had better be no more noise." Or sometimes the teacher can just be quiet and look serious. The authority the teacher carries is seen and working as the children realize their place and know they need to be obedient. The exact words do not matter. What matters is that authority is executed.

This is also true in the spiritual realm. One does not have to say, "I bind you," for example. When casting out a demon, the person can simply command the demon to leave, without saying specific words in a ritual way. Saying, "This demonic spirit of ___ must go," or "All demonic spirits must leave now," or "On three, all of you must go: one, two, three" can all work just the same.

Additionally, the phrase *in Jesus' name* means you are operating and doing these things by Jesus and for His glory. It's good to say "In Jesus' name," but it's not about the words. The demons obey because you walk in true authority that comes from Jesus. The demons tremble because they know the truth that Jesus has sent you. So, at times saying, "You must go now" works just as well as saying, "You must go in Jesus' name."

The point is, you should not think that the process of casting out demons involves a ritual or something specific you recite. It's the authority you carry and walk in that makes demons go.

CAN CHILDREN BE AROUND WHERE DEMONS ARE CAST OUT?

Yes, children can be present when demons are cast out, and they should be! To be where demons are being cast out is the safest place in the world. When demons are cast out, it means the power of God is present! The power of God releases not only miracles that you need for your life but also protection over you. The safest place to be is in the place of surrender. People need to meet Jesus, and they often need to encounter His power to be able to surrender to Him. Being at a gathering where anointing is flowing and demons are being cast out allows you to be at a place where you can experience divine encounters with God that change your life forever. These encounters most often lead people out of the lukewarm life and into total surrender.

Demons are sent by witches and warlocks when a

person opens a door through sin. So, a demon can enter a person in any physical location except a church where God's power is. A person can receive a demon in bed as they sleep with someone outside marriage. A person can receive a demon in their home as they indulge in porn or a horror movie. A person can receive a demon at a club as they take drugs. It's the spiritual door opening that leads to a demon entering.

When a demon leaves a person, such as at church, the demon does not linger, looking for where to go next. When a demon is cast out, it is sent back to the sender (a witch or warlock). At times, God leads His servant to send the demon to the pit in hell. But servants of God cannot send all demons to the pit. According to the laws in the spiritual realm, the devil and demons cannot be terminated at this point in time. People have free will to make their own choices and decisions. Some people through their actions desire demons. They desire to indulge in their sins or access demonic powers to give them things they want.

Because of people's free will and choices, demons are allowed to exist and witches and warlocks are allowed to send them. As servants of God our job is not to eradicate demons but to cast them out of people—out of those who desire Jesus and all that He offers. Our job is not to force deliverance on people who do not want it.

I've seen numerous children, from infants to teenagers, receive deliverance! Children need deliverance just as much as adults do. I've also seen so many children become on fire for Jesus as the result of witnessing deliverance and/or receiving deliverance themselves.

He said, "Leave the children alone, and do not forbid them from coming to Me; for the kingdom of heaven belongs to such as these."
—Matthew 19:14, amp

If I cast out demons with the finger of God, surely the kingdom of God has come upon you.
—Luke 11:20, nkjv

To keep children from being in the church where demons are being cast out is to forbid them from coming to Jesus and experiencing His kingdom. We must become like children to enter the kingdom of God. Children are naturally teachable and prone to understand spiritual principles, because being childlike is the only way to receive the things of the Spirit.

You don't need to worry about your child being frightened when demons manifest. Explain to them the power and beauty of what Jesus is about to do before going to the service. After the service, discuss the miracles and deliverances they witnessed as well. I believe they will be in awe of Jesus and their faith will grow exponentially because of what they witnessed and encountered! Just like the rest of us, children need to witness God's power and experience the kingdom of heaven in their lives.

Conclusion

At this moment God has opened your spiritual eyes and revealed many mysteries of His kingdom. The time for the devil to stay hidden in your life has officially passed! You are equipped to see spiritually and never be fooled by the enemy again. He can no longer bring oppression in your life. With all that you have received in this book, it is now time to go from glory to glory and focus on being who God has called you to be.

You will no longer live in the deficit.

You no longer have to be distracted by oppression and the devil's hold on your life. You are free! You've moved out of the negatives, and now it's time to move beyond zero and into the positives. It's time to walk in abundance!

You have been freed from anxiety and depression. Now it's time to have abundant peace and joy.

You have been freed from demonic dreams. Now it's time to have peaceful, restful sleep.

You were delivered from insomnia and constantly being tired. Now it's time to have supernatural abundant energy and strength.

You were set free from infirmities and healed of sickness, and now it's time to have abundant health and energy.

You were freed from condemnation, and now it's time to experience God's love for you and have intimacy with Him every day.

You were set free from poverty. Now it's time to have an abundance of finances for God's glory and for blessing others, as well as contributing to God's work.

You were set free from so much that has kept you stuck and unable to thrive in life and in your calling. Now it's time to walk in abundance and flourish!

God wants to use you as a vessel of His power. He wants to pour His anointing in you so He can do whatever He pleases through you. Your purpose is to be a vessel of His power. That's the only way you'll be able to fully accomplish the aspects of your specific calling. I have written a book called *The Secret of the Anointing* that releases the secrets of how to access the anointing to walk in miracles. In it you'll discover what God is looking for in a "chosen one"—and what makes someone a trustworthy vessel. Once you've received the anointing, you'll discover how to adequately walk in it as well as how to steward and maintain it. (You can find additional help through my Walking in Miracles e-course at enlivenmedia.org/walking-in-miracles.)

If you want to be equipped to cast out demons and heal the sick, this book you just read holds so many practical tools and keys that will help you as you minister to others. I encourage you to reread this book with a different perspective—a perspective to help others. The practical tools, keys, and principles explained in this book, combined with knowledge of accessing the anointing, will mature you into a trustworthy disciple in the body of Christ. I encourage you to take a step forward and begin walking in your calling by receiving equipping and impartation as you read *The Secret of the Anointing*. And I speak this over you:

> *I declare this anointing to come upon your life now and fill you with abundant joy and peace. May you go from glory to glory from now on. May you walk in abundance now. May blessings and miracles continually flow to you. May nothing take you out of God's will. May you be used by God to lead many people to Jesus. May your testimony of your deliverance lead to many people also receiving freedom! May nothing keep you from moving forward every day, and may nothing keep you from being who God created you to be: a powerful vessel of God! It's time to step into the revival army as an anointed warrior of God!*

Notes

CHAPTER 3: HOW DEMONIC OPPRESSION HAPPENS

1. "Answers to Common Questions: Who Holds the Keys?," Proclaiming the Gospel, accessed December 10, 2024, https://www.proclaimingthegospel.org/page/articles.

CHAPTER 6: HOW TO ACTIVATE FAITH

1. "How Can Jesus and the Bible Both Be the Word of God?," Got Questions, accessed December 11, 2024, https://www.gotquestions.org/Jesus-Bible-Word-God.html.

CHAPTER 7: WHAT MAKES DEMONS GO—KEY 3: RENOUNCING

1. *Oxford Dictionary of English*, 3rd ed., s.v. "renounce," 2010, https://archive.org/details/oxforddictionary0000unse_a2v4/page/1504/mode/2up?view=theater.

CHAPTER 8: THE REALITY OF WITCHCRAFT

1. Melissa Evans Persensky, "What Is Reiki? And Does It Actually Work?," Cleveland Clinic, July 16, 2024, https://health.clevelandclinic.org/reiki.
2. Jennifer Heeren, "What Is 'Manifesting,' and Is It a Sin?," Crosswalk.com, July 11, 2022, https://www.crosswalk.com/faith/spiritual-life/what-is-manifesting-and-is-it-christian.html.
3. Wikipedia, s.v. "yoga," last modified December 13, 2024, 14:38, https://en.wikipedia.org/wiki/Yoga.
4. "Deepen Your Understanding of Yoga With These Important Reads," The Whole U, University of Washington, December 11, 2023, https://thewholeu.uw.edu/2023/12/11/books-with-balance-6-great-yoga-and-meditation-reads/.
5. Jareb Nott, "Kundalini vs. Holy Spirit: Discerning the Deception of Demonic Practices," Destiny Image, June 13, 2024, https://www.destinyimage.com/blog/jareb-nott-kundalini-vs-holy-spirit-discerning-the-deception-of-demonic-practices.

About the Author

ATHRYN KRICK IS the lead pastor of Five-Fold (5F) Church in Los Angeles, where many miracles happen and people receive impartation and are healed, delivered, and transformed by God's power. People travel from all over the world to encounter God at 5F Church weekly. Kathryn has large and rapidly growing YouTube, Facebook, and Instagram audiences where several thousand have received miracles as they watched her live services and videos online. She also travels around the world ministering at revival events, and her greatest passion is to see others encounter God's power and have revelation of His love. Kathryn makes her home in Los Angeles. Find out more about her and about 5F Church at the following:

5fchurch.org

apostlekathrynkrick.com

youtube.com/apostlekathrynkrick

facebook.com/apostlekathrynkrick

instagram.com/apostlekathrynkrick